ALSO BY TOM STONE

Armstrong

Greece: An Illustrated History

Greek Dictionary and Phrasebook

The Essential Greek Handbook

Patmos: A History and Guide

The Summer of
My Greek Tavérna

A Memoir

Tom Stone

SIMON & SCHUSTER
New York   London   Toronto   Sydney   Singapore

SIMON & SCHUSTER
Rockefeller Center
1230 Avenue of the Americas
New York, NY 10020

SIMON & SCHUSTER and colophon are registered trademarks
of Simon & Schuster, Inc.

For information about special discounts for bulk purchases,
please contact Simon & Schuster Special Sales:
1-800-456-6798 or business@simonandschuster.com

Designed by Jan Pisciotta
Maps by Jeff Ward, based on original maps by Tom Stone

Manufactured in the United States of America

1 3 5 7 9 10 8 6 4 2

Library of Congress Cataloging-in-Publication Data
Stone, Tom.
The summer of my Greek tavérna / Tom Stone.
p. cm.
1. Patmos Island (Greece)—Description and travel. 2. Stone, Tom—Journeys—
Greece—Patmos Island. 3. Restaurants—Greece—Patmos Island.
4. Cookery, Greek. I. Title.
DF901.P27 S76 2002
647.95495'87—dc21   2002021209

ISBN 0-7432-0541-3

Acknowledgments

To my agent, Liza Dawson, for her many excellent suggestions during the writing of this book and for her continual faith that I would be able to accomplish what I'd set out to do. To my editor, Sydny Miner, for taking it mostly on faith and for the best and most gentle job of editing I could possibly have imagined. To Dick Wimmer, Mary Hurst, and Maxine Nunes for their crucial creative input and encouragement throughout the writing. To Armistead Maupin for getting it off the ground when it was only an idea born in an airport bookstore, and to Joan Tewksbury for immediately and wholeheartedly falling in love with it.

But most of all, to Florence and Samantha and Oliver, for all the best of reasons.

To

Robert Lax

(1915–2000)

and

the people of Patmos

Author's Note

Recipes for virtually all the dishes mentioned in the story can be found in the "Extra Helpings" section (page 201).

The sometimes rather free translations of Cavafy's poems are wholly my responsibility.

Contents

In the Same Space

Houses, cafés, neighborhoods,
spaces I have seen and walked through
all these years,

you I have created in happiness and sorrow:
in such detail, such detail,

that you are transformed completely into feeling,
for me.

—C. P. CAVAFY

Helen
I never went to Troy; it was a phantom . . .

Servant
What? You mean that it was only for a cloud that
we struggled so much?

—EURIPIDES, *Helen*

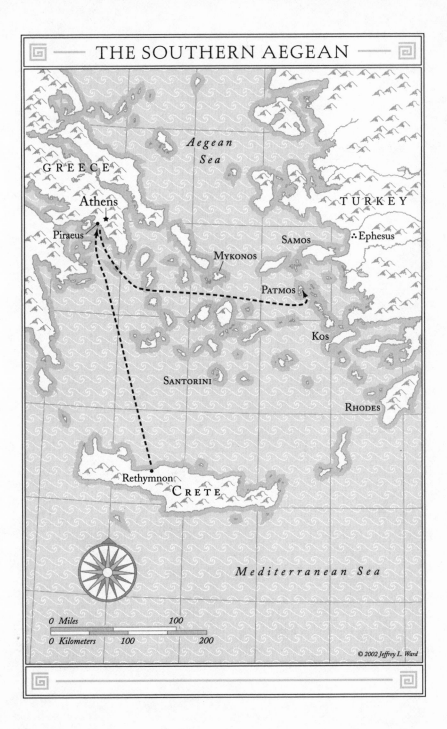

THE SOUTHERN AEGEAN

GREECE

Aegean
Sea

Athens

Piraeus

TURKEY

Ephesus

Samos

Mykonos

Patmos

Kos

Santorini

Rhodes

Rethymnon
CRETE

Mediterranean Sea

0 Miles   100
0 Kilometers   100   200

© 2002 Jeffrey L. Ward

PATMOS

Ághios Nikólas △

Skála

† Monastery of the Apocalypse

Hóra † Monastery of St. John

HILIOMÓDI

Cave of
Yénoupas

0 Miles   1   2

0 Kilometers   2

© 2002 Jeffrey L. Ward

The Summer of
My Greek Tavérna

Preface

If you visit the Greek island of Patmos today, you will not find a restaurant named The Beautiful Helen nor a farming valley and beach called Livádi. These and the names of the people in my story I have changed to protect the privacy of the latter, most of whom are either still living on the island or regularly visiting it.

Nevertheless, the details about Patmos and its legends are all true, as are those about my attempt, one summer not too long ago, to run a tavérna there. In fact, if you go and sit awhile in any small restaurant on the island, you will find that it—and all the other tavérnas throughout Greece, for that matter—is pretty much like The Beautiful Helen. Doubtless, even when St. John first arrived on Patmos in 95 A.D., such a place was already in business, welcoming strangers with open arms, eager to hear their news of the outside world and ready to supply them with a cup of wine and a good bite to eat.

And perhaps at a corner table, there was someone like the man I have called Theológos, waiting to teach them a lesson.

Appetizers

God's Word

The phone rang just as I was about to leave home and trudge through the raw Cretan winter to my tutoring job. The school where I worked was half a mile away, housed in a gray concrete building in the modern part of Rethymnon, along the highway just outside the old city gates. It was a private establishment, a cluster of shabby rooms on the building's second floor, where my Greek colleagues and I would spend each late afternoon and evening teaching English as a Foreign Language. Our pupils were mostly listless civil servants looking to move up the pay scale and high school students hoping for careers as guides, bank clerks, and tourist police. The pay was minimal, and the blackboards sprayed with so many layers of pale green paint that writing on them was often like trying to use chalk on the side of a cargo ship.

My wife, Danielle, answered the phone and called me in out of the rain. When I walked into the living room, she was holding the receiver in one hand and a delicate, shimmering sheet of gold leaf in the other. The gold leaf was for a Byzantine icon she was painting, one of a line of copies she hoped to sell to local tourist shops. Eight-and-a-half years before, when we met on the island of Patmos, she had been doing the same thing, a temporary measure on the way to realizing her dream of creating her own work. Now that we had two children to support, she was back at it again, just as I was learning to teach instead of working on a new novel. She had seemed able to easily accept this, shrugging it off with typical French stoicism. American that I was, I was still struggling, even at forty-two, to believe that downsizing my dreams and taking on a steady job again was a good thing.

She pressed the mouthpiece against her upper arm. "It's Theológos."

In a corner of the living room our two towheaded children—Sara, six, and Matt, going on two—were playing with the cat, sitting next to the cast-iron stove we huddled around in the afternoons and evenings while waiting for heat to drift down to us from the distant mildewed ceiling. When we had rented this apartment in the old city—four cavernous rooms on the second floor of a crumbling, marble-porticoed, seventeenth-century Venetian mansion—we thought it was a steal. Now, in our second winter in Rethymnon, we knew who had done the stealing, and that it was the landlord, not us.

"Theológos?" I asked.

"From Patmos. Livádi."

I looked at her with surprise. Although we had lived in the Patmos farming valley of Livádi winter and summer for more than seven years, buying and restoring a house there, the last people we ever expected to hear from again were its inhabitants. Even more insular than other Patmians, they referred to the people from its port, five miles away, as *xéni*, foreigners. They also regarded the telephone as a useful but dangerously extravagant device and rarely used it, particularly long distance.

"*O Ladós?*" I said, using his nickname—a necessity on Patmos, where it seemed that half the men were named either Theológos or Ioánnis (for short, "Yánnis") in honor of St. John the Theologian, *Ághios Ioánnis O Theológos*. It was on Patmos that John had received the visions that were set down in the Book of Revelations, in Greek, *ee Apokálypsi*—the Apocalypse.

Theh-ós means God, and *lógos* word or reason; thus, *theológos*—*theologian* or God's word.

Danielle nodded.

Theológos owned a ramshackle but thriving restaurant on Livádi Beach. Not really a restaurant, but what the Greeks call a *tavérna*—smaller and less expensive than a regular restaurant (*estiatórion*) and usually family-run. When I first arrived on the island, it had been called *Ee Oráya Eléni* (The Beautiful Helen), but a year later, Eléni, his wife, left him, taking their daughter with her, and Theológos cut down the tree outside and changed the name to *Ee Oráya Théa*—The Beautiful View—which it certainly had. Sitting on the road that ran parallel to the sea, it looked through a cluster of tamarisk trees to a sand-and-pebble beach and a wide, curving bay where brightly painted fishing boats—caïques—bobbed upon the shifting, glittering waters. In the distance rose the graceful slopes of Hiliomódi, a small offshore island used by goatherders. Beyond that could be seen the shadowy shapes of other islands in the Dodecanese and, in the sharp light of winter, even the amaranthine undulations of the Turkish coast forty miles away.

Danielle handed me the phone and went back to her table, delicately applying the gold leaf to the surface of the icon she was working on. She was thirty-two and her body, even in a bulky winter sweater and after two children, was as slim as a twenty-year-old's. As she bent over the icon, her auburn hair fell across her face, and her fine French cheekbones, sloe eyes, and slightly aquiline nose were taut with concentration. The children had inherited their blond hair from the Scandinavian side of my family, but the beautiful delicacy of their features was entirely their mother's.

"Theológo!" I said into the telephone, using the Greek form of address in which the final "*s*" is cut off. "How are you?!"

Theológos wasn't much for small talk. An ex-merchant seaman, a *capitánios*, he claimed, who had meandered all over the world, he now liked to get straight to the point. Particularly long distance. So as soon as he heard my voice, he weighed anchor and set sail, hardly giving me a chance to say hello.

"Thomá!" he shouted, trumpeting the Greek version of my name all the way from Patmos. "Listen! You want to rent my tavérna this summer?"

Theológos. God's word.

The Beautiful Helen

"Thomá, are you there?" He was still on the line, waiting for me to answer, his voice crackling and faint. In bad winter weather, there was a constant possibility of being cut off, particularly when calling from one island to another. "Thomá, listen! The man from Athens—the one who rented it two years ago?—wants it again, but I thought of you. Always you told me, if you had my tavérna. Remember?"

I remembered. His offer had instantly conjured up visions of The Beautiful Helen (I was unable to imagine it with any other name), which now beguilingly arose in my mind's eye like glittering Aphrodite shining from the sea. I remembered those early summer mornings seated at a table by the beach sipping a Greek coffee, breathing in the smell of the tamarisk trees and listening to the soft slap of waves against the side of a caïque; the lazy oregano-scented lunches, after which Danielle and I would go back to our house to take a nap within the wonderful coolness of our thick-walled farmhouse and, with the children asleep, perhaps make love; and those evenings when the outside world narrowed down to the few yards illuminated by the tavérna's lights and that mad exhilaration, which the Greeks call *kéfi*, descended upon the gathering like a tongue of fire . . .

The Beautiful Helen was one of those restaurants you come

across in Greece and sit in and absolutely know that you can do a better job of running than its present owner. Put some bamboo here and there, soft lighting for the evening, install better toilets, get yourself a couple of waiters who care about what they're doing, whip up some interesting recipes, and most of all, serve the food *hot*. The location will take care of the rest.

So, a few years before, when Theológos had begun leasing out his place for the season rather than suffer through what was becoming an increasing crush of tourists, I started saying, "You should rent it to me!"

This had been an idle request. Though I was a dedicated amateur cook and had worked in a restaurant once before, my offer was often also fueled by an excess of retsina and *kéfi*. Theológos himself had known this, and laughed along with me. Now, however, he was taking me seriously.

I looked at my watch. I could afford perhaps another five minutes before my trudge to the tutoring school would have to become a dash.

Out of curiosity, I asked, "How much?"

This immediately got Danielle's attention.

There was a pause before Theológos answered. "The man from Athens offered three hundred fifty thousand," he said. "For you, I can make it three hundred thousand drachmas, but no less."

About seven thousand dollars.

"Theológo, even if I wanted to, I don't have that kind of money."

Danielle stared at me.

"I thought you sold your house," said Theológos.

This caught me off guard. "Where did you hear that?"

"*Eémay Patmiótis!* I'm a Patmian! Everybody knows everybody else's business here. You sold your house, yes? To the Dutch doctor whose daughter wants it for her dowry?"

Amazing.

"Yes," I replied. "But," I lied, "we still haven't been paid. And we're planning to put the money away for the children. For their future. College . . ."

Now even the kids were listening. At least Sara was, while Matt just sat there happily trying to pull the fur off the cat's back.

"Ah! Well, then . . ." Theológos answered, raking in his chips.

Friends of mine who owned restaurants on the island of Mykonos had told me they made enough money in one summer to last them the entire year. And at that moment, they were probably spending the winter in Paris or New York, seeing the shows, eating at the best restaurants, while I . . .

"Theológo, wait. Let me think it over."

Danielle now began to look more than a little alarmed. I couldn't blame her. She knew I had a genetic predisposition, inherited from my late father, an architect and real estate developer in Washington, D.C., for formulating grandiose projects. While this tendency had brought me to Greece in the first place and had eventually gotten us our farmhouse on Patmos, she also knew that when my father died, he had been seventy thousand dollars in debt, mostly to his bookie.

"Thomá!" Theológos was shouting over the phone, "*Élla!* Come! Everybody misses you! You're one of us—*Patmiótis!*"

The line went dead.

Patmiótis

One of the first things people want to know is how you do it— how you can just pull up stakes on your career (I had been a Broadway stage manager and fledgling director) and go off and live on a Greek island. The thing is, you don't really plan to.

Practically all the foreigners I know who have ended up living in Greece for any extended period of time say the same thing: *"I just went for a few weeks [days/hours]. But then . . ."*

But then, something happens. Like love.

All I had wanted was to spend the summer there, four or five months at the most, and live out a long-held dream I'd cherished of going away somewhere and writing a novel. My mother had recently died of a stroke and had left me a small legacy. I put ten thousand dollars of it away in a desultory stock market, and took the rest, about two thousand, and left for Greece, where I had a painter friend, Dick Evans, also a former Broadway stage manager, who would help me get acclimated. I was thirty-three and figured I should get this out of my system before it was too late, before I married and had children—*"The full catastrophe!"* as Zorba says.

"I'll be back at the end of the summer," I told my friends.

※

I arrived in Greece on a bright, windswept day in March. After short stays in Athens and on the island of Mykonos, where I learned more about the *hasápiko* (Zorba's dance) than I did about my writing talents, I decided that if I were to get any work done at all, I would have to find some place far away from the siren calls that await you along the beaten tourist track.

I chose Patmos as the designated island by simply closing my eyes and dropping my finger on a map of the Aegean, fully confident that now that I was in Greece, I was in the hands of a benevolent Fate who would see to it that all would be well, no matter where my finger landed. "But Patmos?!" I asked. Dick hadn't heard of it either.

An old *Fodor's Guide to Greece* that I had found in the Athens flea market had little to say about the island. Seven miles long and three wide, it was a speck at the edge of the eastern Aegean, one of a scattering of islands along the Turkish coast known as the Dodecanese, ten hours by ship from Athens's port of Piraeus in the northwest and exactly the same from the island of Rhodes to the south. Ships rarely went there, however, because of the lack of a pier large enough for them to dock at. The guide also had some cursory information on St. John and the Book of Revelations, and a grainy black-and-white photograph of the harbor showing a few grayish-white houses and gray rocks merging into a gray sea under a cloudless gray sky. Well, I thought, I'll try it out. If it doesn't work, I can always go on to the next one.

So, at 6 A.M. on a clear morning at the beginning of May, I stumbled out onto the deck of a battered old ferryboat, the now immortal *Miméka*, for my first view of Patmos, completely unprepared for the revelation awaiting me. Gone were the gray skies, gray rocks, and gray sea. Instead, the rising sun was turning the high, jagged sandstone rocks of its coastline into a rich amber, and the slopes of its hills and valleys were covered with a glowing patina of green from the winter rains. In the distance, tiny caïques were making their way toward us from harbor, cutting through the sparkling blue water. Most of the passengers were looking in that direction and at the dark, brooding, crenellated mass of the Monastery of St. John on a hill to the south of the harbor, but something drew my attention to the north, where I could see a sprinkling of white-washed farmhouses nestled in a distant emerald valley. "There!" said a little voice inside me. "You want to go there!" "There," I would later learn, was Livádi.

The dock that we disembarked on from our caïque was little more than the stone-buttressed side of a dirt road that ran along the harbor, a step above the water's edge. Skála, the name of the port town, was the same as the Greek word for "step," and this was probably the reason why it had been called simply that. In fact, the docking facilities looked as if they hadn't changed all that much since St. John first stepped off his caïque on that journey from Ephesus almost two thousand years before.

Except, that is, for the huge concrete blocks that lay jumbled at one end of the harbor. Recently, the government in Athens had decided to show Turkey how possessive it was of the Dodecanese and had begun constructing not only a new pier on Patmos but, later, an army encampment and seaside pillboxes as well.

In the harbor, a rusted dredging barge sat dormant in the water, waiting for a more seemly hour to begin its clangorous day-long operations preparing the sea bottom for the concrete blocks.

Near the middle of the harbor a bright red buoy bobbed upon the waters, about fifty yards from the western shoreline. This, I would later learn, marked the spot where a dangerously jagged rock capable of ripping open the hull of a large ship lay just beneath the surface. It was—and is—believed to be the petrified form of Yénoupas, an evil *mágus* turned to stone by St. John in a battle for the hearts, minds, and souls of the island's inhabitants.

This battle is not yet over—as I was reminded again and again during my stay on the island—and the story of the encounter between John and Yénoupas, a purely local legend, tells so much about Patmos that it is worth recounting here and now.

St. John and the Mágus

In A.D. 95, John was living in Ephesus with Mary, the mother of Jesus, when the order came down from the emperor Domitian to send him into exile.

"*I, John,*" he wrote in the Book of Revelations, "*was on Patmos because I had preached God's word and borne my testimony to Jesus.*"

One of the legends about his stay, depicted on frescoes in the Monastery of St. John, says that during the voyage from Ephesus (nowadays about a six-hour trip by caïque and twenty minutes in a hydrofoil, but back then, probably a day or more), a sudden storm swept one of the passengers overboard. He seemed lost until John raised his manacled hands to the heavens and made the sign of the cross. Immediately, the drowning man was deposited back on board by another wave. As a result, by the time the still-shackled John arrived at Skála, he was once again at his calling, preaching the good news of Jesus to a boatload of now-converted fellow travelers.

The story of these miracle-working powers prompted the Roman governor of the island to seek John's help in releasing his brother-in-law from some sort of demonic possession. In short order, John exorcised the demon and added the governor and his entire family to his list of converts, moving in to live with the governor's father-in-law and, freed from his shackles, establishing his new home as Patmos's first Christian house of worship.

These events so alarmed the priests of the island's Apollonian cult that they sought help from a sorcerer named Yénoupas, who lived in a sulfurous cave on the desolate southwestern edge of the island.* Yénoupas promptly journeyed to town to discredit this interloper from Ephesus.

---

* This cave still exists, reeking of volcanic fumes and so warm that a hermit is said to have lived within it for fifty-five years with only a low wall to protect him in winter. A precarious footpath used to lead there, and I have spoken to Patmians who dared the trip as youths. But the mountain in which it is housed is gradually being demolished by a gravel-mining company, and in a few years, it may be entirely destroyed—unless, of course, public awareness is raised by protests such as this one.

In Skála, he publicly challenged John to a contest of magical powers. When John refused, Yénoupas showed his disdain by diving into the harbor and raising from its depths the effigies of three dead Patmians. Mightily impressed with this display of power, the watching crowd of Patmians turned on John, berating and then beating him so badly that he was left for dead.

Miraculously, John survived. Upon hearing this, Yénoupas returned to finish the job. As another crowd gathered, Yénoupas again leapt into the harbor. This time, however, John called on God to help him—as He had helped Moses defeat the pagan god Amalek—by turning Yénoupas to stone before he could rise from the waters.

With a sudden roar, a whirlpool formed over the spot where Yénoupas had disappeared, and he was immediately petrified, imprisoned forever beneath the harbor waters.

Afterward, John remained on the island in relative freedom and peace and quiet for another year or so. In September 96, the emperor Domitian was assassinated and his edicts revoked, thus allowing John to return to Ephesus. Before he departed, the Patmians asked him to write down his teachings about Jesus for them, so he and his scribe, Próchorus, retired to a secluded hillside cave overlooking the harbor. While there, it is said that John not only wrote his gospel but received the dark visions that are recorded in the Book of Revelations. As he and Próchorus were sitting in the cave, its roof split open and *"a great voice, as of a trumpet, said, 'I am Alpha and Omega, the first and the last and what thou seest, write in a book.'"*

After having Próchorus transcribe his visions, John returned to Ephesus, where it is believed he was buried.

A thousand years later, the Monastery of St. John was raised in his honor, and the island has since become a renowned repository of priceless Christian artifacts, of numerous documents, paintings, and miracle-working relics, including an icon of St. John, which has several times saved Patmos from both natural and man-made disasters.

Nevertheless, the dark, apocalyptic shadow of Yénoupas continues to loom over the island, and although petrified, he is not without power.

When the Italians were occupying the Dodecanese from 1912 to 1948, they tried to rip out the rock with a dredger, but the force of the effort threw the ship, not the rock, out of the waters. Later, an enterprising Patmian unsuccessfully attempted to dynamite it. The following day, he was repaid for his efforts with a fatal heart attack.

And so, even during the construction of this massive new pier with all the resources of modern technology, the rock of Yénoupas had been given a wide berth. And even the most casual visitor can still detect, in the island's seeming air of sanctity, a definite whiff of menace.

The Ruins of Hóra

At the time of my arrival, the route of the island's creaking, antiquated bus effectively divided Patmos into three areas: the central sea-level port of Skála and its neighboring merchant communities; the hilltop administrative capital of Hóra to the south; and to the north, the valleys, plains, and coves of Patmos's various farming and fishing communities, including Livádi.

Skála was the place where everyone converged to bring their goods to market, to shop, to go to the doctor's, the dentist's, and to the post and telegraph offices. Made up of a cluster of modest, whitewashed buildings curving around the harbor, Skála had a narrow beach lined with tamarisk trees on one side, a blue-domed whitewashed church on the other, and in its center, an incongruous Italianate customs building, the last remnant of that strange occupation that began during the dismemberment of the Ottoman Empire and that lasted through World War II.

There were several minuscule grocery stores, a couple of bakeries and butcher shops, and a vegetable market displaying the sad fruits of an island whose water supply was reduced to a low trickle by the end of August. A few fishermen's boats lined that part of the old harbor that was still usable, and three over-the-hill taxis awaited infrequent customers in the shade of the customs house.

I found someone who spoke English. His name was Chrístos, and he was the owner of a travel agency, which he operated out of his late father's sweet shop. I asked about places to rent, about that valley I had seen to the north. "No, no," he said, "there's nothing to rent out there. Go to Hóra. A wonderful place! You will love it. All the foreigners love it! They buy houses there! The bus is leaving right now. Go! I promise you, you'll love it!" As I grabbed my bag and ran toward the bus, he shouted after me: "The view is wonderful!"

It was not only wonderful, it was breathtaking. As I got off the bus at the top of the hill, eight hundred feet up, I was treated to a magnificent panorama of the island, whose undulating hills and valleys spread out toward the north in a multitude of coves and bays, some of them sprinkled with tiny white houses, and one of them, on the eastern side, the valley I had seen from the *Miméka*. Farther to the north, across an expanse of silvery water, was the long length of the island of Samos, and to the right, the coast of Turkey, from which John had sailed to Patmos, to exile and the word of God.

Behind me, the Monastery of St. John jutted out of the mounting cubist jumble of whitewashed houses that was Hóra. I began walking up the steep, stone-paved incline that led into town, ignoring the signs pointing the way to the monastery, and heading instead into the labyrinthine interior.

Soon, there were massive stone walls rising on either side of me, the few windows that were in them barred and shuttered, their wooden doors thick with molding and grillwork. These were not just houses but magnificent mansions, most two and three stories tall, a few with arcaded terraces on their upper floors. Many were clearly deserted, their walls crumbled and spilling out into the streets, exposing long-neglected gardens high with weeds and the barbed husks of last year's brambles.

For the longest while, I didn't see a single person, although the occasional flutter of a lace curtain in a doorway or window betrayed a living presence somewhere. As the streets meandered up and down, through covered passageways and lanes so strait that you lost all sense of where the sun was, I began to feel like Kafka's land surveyor K. in his search for that mysteriously unattainable castle. What was a town like this, obviously once so wealthy, doing on such a supposedly austere monastic outpost as Patmos?

Later I would learn that both the wealth and the devastation were the result of the acquisitiveness of the monks, as well as the island's lay population, most of the latter Cretans originally imported to build the monastery. In the sixteenth century, taking advantage of Patmos's tax-exempt status as a holy island, they would join forces to assemble, for God and for themselves, one of the most profitable mercantile fleets in the Mediterranean. The mansions were one result of this burgeoning prosperity, as were the maze of streets designed to confuse invaders. Another was the continuing accumulation of treasures within the monastery.

Of course, such wealth inevitably attracted the attention of Arab pirates and the warships of European and Balkan powers. Soon the island was being repeatedly attacked and, finally, badly pillaged. Completing the destruction were two massive earthquakes, the last of which was followed by two months of continual aftershocks. In the nineteenth century, Greece's successful war of independence from the Turks resulted in Patmos and its obsolete sailing ships being yoked to the carcass of the dying Ottoman Empire. Thereafter, much of what remained was abandoned and left in ruins.

By the time I finally emerged from the warren of Hóra's streets into a tiny square with a café, I knew that this was not the place for me. Aside from the eerie emptiness, it was too far from the sea and the earth. Too much like a city. And then there were the foreigners that Chrístos had spoken about. They were up here somewhere, no doubt living sumptuously in houses they had bought and then renovated for a song. I didn't want to get to know them, didn't want to suffer through the envy I would feel when I saw their homes. Besides, there would be no time for socializing. I had only a summer to work on the novel, and I intended to live like a monk.

Anyway, my little voice was still telling me to go out to that valley.

Livadiótis

Back in Skála, I found a taxi driver to take me to Livádi. His name was Evripídes and he was the proud and loving possessor of a heavily chromed, pastel-green 1950s Buick, whose full-throated rumblings had led him to call it *"toh aeropláno mou,"* "my airplane." Evripídes was from Livádi—a *Livadiótis*—and he thought there was a small possibility I might find something to rent. Anyway, I had to see his valley. It was the most beautiful place on Patmos!

The dusty dirt road curved above the coastline for about five miles, providing glimpses of several other bays to the east and west before arriving at the tiny village of Upper Livádi, a collection of one-story stone houses, a small grocery, a pair of rudimentary cafés, and a large church. From there, it was a steep half-mile descent into the valley along a road so badly gutted by winter rains that Evripídes had to slow to a near halt to guide his precious *aeropláno* through the turbulence of the gullies.

The valley was indeed beautiful—spreading out below us like an amphitheater, sloping sharply down to a wide alluvial plain that was crisscrossed with low stone walls, donkey paths, and nearly dry riverbeds. Masses of cacti sprouted out of the rocky hillsides, and fig, lemon, and olive trees blossomed the landscape. Farmhouses and roughly built animal enclosures rose from the earth as if grown there—out of the hillsides, in nooks against the rocks, and in groups on the lower plain, while a few tiny whitewashed churches dotted the stonewalled paths that wound between the fields.

At the foot of the valley to the east was a wide horseshoe-shaped bay with a beach nearly spanning its entire five-hundred-yard length. In the middle, a small stone pier jutted out into the sea, and a few fishermen's caïques were anchored between it and the southern headland. Along the beachfront road, tiny, single-story residences sat beneath clusters of tamarisk trees.

"Maybe there," said Evripídes.

It was as if I had been holding my breath for a long, long time and hadn't even realized it. Not until, at the sight of this valley, I could feel it slowly begin to release.

There are places that seem to be waiting for you out there somewhere, like unmet lovers, and when (and if) you come upon them, you know, instantly and unquestioningly, that they are the ones. It is as if, far back in time, there had been an intimate connection to that very spot or person. So it was with Livádi. Even from as far away as the deck of the *Miméka*, it had been love at first sight. I knew that there I would find not simply a house to rent but a place to belong to. Like Odysseus, I felt as if I were coming home to Ithaca after a long voyage through the troubled waters of foreign lands (including my birthplace) whose languages I had never really understood.

And it still amazes me to think that at that very moment, on another part of Patmos, in a little house on a cove that I had passed on the road to Livádi, the future mother of my children was sitting on her terrace pondering, as I was, what she was really going to do with her life now that she had finally gotten here.

Danielle

I hung up the telephone. "The line's dead."

"What did Theológos want?" asked Danielle.

"Nothing," I said dismissively. "He has some crazy idea about renting me the tavérna for the summer."

And off I ran to work.

By the time I returned in the evening, I had that slightly queasy thrill in my stomach that I get when I'm about to do something that goes totally against every bit of common sense I have. I was becoming obsessed with Theológos's offer. The problem now would be convincing Danielle.

Her father, in sharp contrast to mine, was a model of prudence. A professor of economics at the university in Aix-en-Provence, he wore suits even on weekend mornings, drove mid-range Citroëns wearing gloves, and put whatever extra money he had into government bonds and blue-chip stocks. Danielle's mother had a degree in anthropology. She had learned Portuguese and had been intending to go to Brazil to study the native Indians when she met this handsome young lawyer and subordinated her career to his. Danielle, in turn, had dutifully gone to the Sorbonne and was working toward a law degree when suddenly she announced to her stunned parents and five brothers and sisters that she had always wanted to be a painter. Without waiting for their reply, she dropped out of law school and enrolled in the École des Beaux Arts.

There she became enamored of the great Russian masters of icon painting and spent a summer studying their techniques at a Russian Orthodox monastery in the South of France. Afterward, she fled continuing family pressures to do the expected and responsible, and following a stint living on the beaches of Crete, had headed for Patmos for the same reasons I had—to see if she really was an artist, or just another dabbler.

The first time I caught sight of her that first summer on Patmos, she was sitting in a café in a side street off the harbor—twenty-three years old, her nut-brown body slim and braless, long auburn hair streaked with gold, and eyes green and almond-shaped—deep in thought, paint-stained fingers picking bits of tobacco off her lips as she stared into space. It was morning, and an ouzo with water in it sat on the table next to her, white as a glass of milk. She was French and full of mystery, and her desire to be left alone had mesmerized all of the men on the island. With that first glimpse of her, I was now included among them. I began to look for her every time I came to the port, hoping for an opportunity to get to know her. But it would be almost the end of the summer before this really happened—and when it did, it would be near chance, or, as I like to say, fate. Typical of those heady days, it had to do with an attempt, at a party at Theológos's tavérna, to walk on water. But we'll get to that later.

Since then, however, Danielle had changed. It had started with her first pregnancy. As soon as Sara was on the way, the occasional morning ouzo had stopped. So had the cigarettes, at least during the length of her pregnancies. And words like "choice" and "responsibility" had begun creeping into her vocabulary, as in: "We chose to have the children. Now it's our responsibility to provide for them."

When I told her how tempting I found Theológos's offer, she came right to the point.

"You are crazy."

I had my arguments ready, however, having been stockpiling them since I'd started off for school that afternoon.

The potential profits could be enormous. I told her about my friends on Mykonos, how they had made enough in one season to last an entire year, at least tripling their investment. If we could work hard for three months every summer, then we would be free to paint and write for the other nine. It was the perfect solution. A hell of a lot better than slaving away in the sweatshop of English as a Second Language and toiling over a production line of tourist-trade icons.

She looked at me. "Patmos isn't Mykonos," she said.

"With the new pier, it can be." I reminded her of our last summer there, how we had hardly been able to find a place to sit at Theológos's, it had been so full.

"In July and August," she reminded me. "Not the entire season. And only in the daytime. What are you going to do at night? There's no bus and it's seven kilometers to the port. I know Mykonos. It's at night they really make their money."

"If we make ours the best on the island," I said, "and that's not hard, people will come."

There would be virtually no competition. All the other restaurants, in Skála and in Hóra, were typical Greek establishments serving the same tired dishes year after year, barely warmed-over *moussaká, pastítsio,* and *tomátes yemistéss* so sodden with oil and cheap margarine that their juices would congeal in the wind before you had a chance to take a bite. Already I was beginning to picture my menu: the old favorites that dinner guests had raved about over the years—Spaghetti alla Carbonara (page 214), Steak au Poivre (page 222), Chinese Chicken with Cucumbers (page 228), Mussel Paella (page 212) . . .

"And our Swiss francs?" said Danielle.

This was her major worry: to rent The Beautiful Helen we would have to change precious foreign currency from the sale of our house into drachmas. Did we want to do this? And what would we do with the profits afterward, if there were any? Greek drachmas were nearly worthless in the outside world, exchangeable for a pittance of their value within the country.

Outside our window, huge droplets of rain continued to fall, their heavy splatter echoing along the narrow, glistening streets of Rethymnon. In my mind, all of those freezing winter nights we had spent in our Livádi farmhouse shivering under clammy sheets and blankets had disappeared. To me, now, on Patmos it had always been summer.

"It will be a one-time investment," I said. "After that, we can pay for the rent every season with the drachmas we made the previous year. And live on the rest during the winter. If we're careful, it can work. For years!"

Along with mentally planning my menu, I was also busily imagining the articles that would be written about us in *Travel & Leisure* and *Gourmet*, picturing the yachts that would anchor in Livádi Bay: *"Yes,"* their owners would say, *"we heard about you and specially sailed over for the evening from Mykonos."*

I pointed at the workspace Danielle had created for herself along the far wall of our bedroom. Two sawhorses supported a messy pressboard plank hardly large enough to hold the crowded jumble of cans and bottles and jars and paper bags containing the brushes, solutions, and powders she used in her work. On the floor was a pile of worm-eaten wood, flotsam and jetsam tossed up by the sea or found in the yards and flooring of abandoned houses, each riddled with twisted rusty nails that would have to be tortuously extracted before she could even begin to paint. On the shelf above the painting area, a line of icons—St. George and the Dragon, the Archangel Michael, Jesus Pantocrator, the Virgin with Child, St. John the Theologian—were lined up in various stages of completion, heading for their final coating of crackling varnish before they would be carried to the tourist shops and the always unpleasant and sometimes nasty bargaining about how much she would be paid and when. In another corner, the elegant portable easel which I bought her on an extravagant trip to New York in anticipation of selling my second novel leaned against the wall, unused.

"Do you want to continue doing this?!" I asked.

"I don't mind."

"What about your own painting?"

She shrugged. "We have the children."

For the past two and a half years, we had been wandering in a slough of failed expectations, often terrified of how we were going to get enough money simply to pay the rent. We had initially come to Crete to have our second child, and the day after his birth, the entire edifice of our financial structure had suddenly come crashing down. That was when I received a letter from my agent in New York telling me to give up hopes that she would be able to sell my second novel.

To survive the rest of the summer, I took a job as a waiter and occasional cook in a tiny, six-table restaurant in Rethymnon. Its owner's name was Socrátes, and he paid me about five dollars a day in tips, plus free food for the family. Then one of our Cretan patrons offered me a full-time job teaching English in his tutoring school. We returned to Patmos to pack up our things. It was there, when we were emptying our coin jar to gather enough money for the trip back to Rethymnon, that we faced the stark realization that our seven-year idyll on the island was over, that with two children to take care of (one already needing schooling), we shouldn't, we *couldn't,* stay even if we had the money. Shortly afterward, we put the farmhouse up for sale. It had taken us nearly two years to restore it, and we had lived in it for only nine months.

But the departure had been too abrupt, and the thread that the Fates had been spinning for us in Patmos didn't feel fully played out. I, for one, needed closure. Renting the tavérna would give me the chance to make one last grand gesture and live this particular dream through to the end I was now envisioning. In a way, we would be—*I* would be—hosting what might be our own summer-long farewell party at The Beautiful Helen.

In addition, there was that twenty-five thousand dollars we had received for the house now resting in our very own Swiss bank account. It had finally been deposited there the month before and had been burning a hole in my pocket ever since as I pondered ways of investing it.

"Money makes money," I said to Danielle. "If we let it sit, we'll eat away at it until there's nothing left. You have to risk something to gain something."

"But seven thousand dollars!"

"I'll tell him I can't do it for that. I'll bargain him down."

Danielle looked out the window at the rain falling on the lamplit streets, down at her paint-flecked fingers, and then back at me. In the other room, Matt and Sara were sleeping.

"Well," she shrugged, "it's your money." Then she smiled. "But just remember why they call him *O Ladós.*"

I did.

In Greek, *ladó* is the root for *oil. Ládi* means oil of any kind, machine, olive, etc. In Livádi, the story went that when Theológos was about five years old, he stole some olive oil from his mother and tried to exchange it in the local grocery store for candy. To this day, some fifty-five years later, he was still known to his fellow islanders as *O Ladós,* "the oily one."

O Ladós

I remembered the first time I had seen Theológos on that afternoon nine years before when Evripídes had taken me out in his taxi to show me Livádi.

He was on the beach in front of the tavérna, carefully administering a final coat of paint to his dry-docked, blue-and-white caïque, the *Pandóra.* A battered Panama fedora was perched on the back of his head and a heavy growth of stubble spread out from his graying Clark Gable mustache. His trousers were rolled up to his knees and a dirty, sweat-stained undershirt covered his slightly hairy and somewhat paunchy upper body. The skin on his face, neck, and forearms was burnt a cinnamon brown, while his upper body and pencil legs were as white and virginal as a baby's.

As Evripídes glided his *aeropláno* in for a dusty landing beside the tavérna, Theológos turned to look up at us, his sharp brown eyes quickly measuring my importance as I stepped out of the cab. It's not too difficult to imagine what he must have thought of me, some sort of hippie left over from the sixties, with longish blond hair, faded Levi's, and brand-new Mykonos sandals. On the other hand, I couldn't have been that badly off because I had had the wherewithal to take a taxi to get there. Whatever, I was the first foreigner of the season to venture all the way out to Livádi Beach and therefore a most welcome diversion, deserving of attention if for no other reason than that.

In no time at all, he had his two bright-eyed sons, Sávas, six, and Lámbros, five, setting up a table and chairs for us under the huge tamarisk tree that then shaded the tavérna's terrace. His

daughter, eleven-year-old Theodóra, shyly cleaned off the
table, her dark eyes taking us in while seemingly never looking
up from her work. Theológos disappeared inside, and the three
children brought out ouzo, glasses, and a modest tray of
mezédes—bread, boiled eggs, olives, canned *dolmádes* (stuffed
vine leaves), and the salt-encrusted pickled bonito known as
lakérda. Theológos's wife, Eléni, remained in the kitchen, only
dimly visible through the weathered panes of Plexiglas that
formed part of the tavérna's winter frontage. Theológos then
reappeared, decked out in a clean white shirt, and joined us for
our ouzo, his hands washed but still spattered with blue.

It was immediately clear that this was no country bumpkin.
If not exactly a man of the world, he had been around. A captain, he said in rudimentary English, on a freighter that plied
the seven seas, from Amsterdam to Macao and South America
and back. And the United States, too. "Hooston," he announced. "Galveston."

Evripídes glanced at me, said, *"Pardón,"* and then com-
menced a rapid-fire exchange in Greek with Theológos. Afterward, Theológos regarded me with renewed interest.

"No houses," he said, wagging his finger. "Rooms, okay, I
can rent you a room, but a house, no."

I opened my arms and spread them questioningly to my
right and left. Along the road were a line of shuttered dwellings
whose overgrown gardens and badly stained whitewash made
them look as though they hadn't been occupied since World
War II. "Many houses," I said. "Nobody there."

Theológos smiled. He then took us out on the beach, where
we could look up and down the full length of the road and
through the line of trees back into the valley. He explained that
all the vacant houses that we saw—and there were many of
them—belonged to Patmian families who had been coming to
summer in Livádi from Hóra or Athens and even Australia for

ages, generations. And even if they weren't coming, they would never rent out their homes. For instance, there was the Comnénus family, descendants of a line of Byzantine emperors, whose two surviving members, an elderly brother and sister, lived in Hóra and had had a summer house in Livádi since the nineteenth century, but never came anymore and never rented it.

So it seemed as though the little voice that had whispered "There!" to me with such insistence had been wrong.

But then I looked farther back in the valley and saw a single-story house, with perhaps two rooms, sitting on a hill, a rocky bluff, in its center, just before the land began to rise upward to the village. It had a terrace out front and its shutters were closed. It practically shouted, "I'm the one!"

I pointed out the house to Theológos, relatively easy to do because of the way it sat up there on its little hill, a forest of cacti sprouting out behind it on either side.

"What about that place?"

"No," said Theológos without a moment's hesitation. "It's a *príka*, a dowry, and their daughter and her husband and daughter come from Athens every summer for two months. Not possible." Evripídes nodded his agreement.

I looked so crestfallen that Theológos slapped me on the back and offered me another ouzo on the house. "I rent you a room for only eleven hundred drachmas a month." He pointed at the curve in the road leading up to the village. "Over there. Near the beach. What do you say?"

I glanced at Evripídes. The expression on his face, recently so animated, had turned utterly blank.

Still, I thought, quickly calculating, thirty-two dollars a month! But I wanted a house. And I wanted that house, the one on the little hill or bluff. I told Theológos I'd let him know the following day.

As Evripídes and I drove up toward the village, he said that

Theológos was trying to cheat me, that a thousand drachmas was too much. He, Evripídes, had a room in Skála that he could give me for only seven hundred and fifty a month. I answered that I wanted to live out here in Livádi, that I intended look some more tomorrow, and then we would talk.

From the road I could see the house that had called to me so strongly from the beach. But now it just sat there on its bluff, shuttered and lonely, staring away from me toward the darkening sea.

Bargaining

For Greeks, bargaining is like breathing. They thrive on it. It is oxygen for their self-esteem, and they seem versed in it from birth. The bloodlines they have in this area are nothing short of awesome. Think about Socrates and his dialogues. The subject matter may be of philosophic concern, but what he's really engaged in is bargaining. He and the gentleman he's talking to start with what seems to be a reasonable, mutually agreeable proposition, but by the time Socrates is finished with him, the man has been thoroughly fleeced and—what's even worse—is *thanking* Socrates for having done it. Add to this the mental agility and survival instincts sharpened in the Greeks by four hundred years of occupation by the Ottoman Turks (not to mention the Levantine marketplace smarts of *that* group), and you've got a race of people you never want to go one on one with, not even for the price of a postcard.

We Americans on the other hand—the solid middle- and lower-class majority of us, anyway, who pledged allegiance to the flag and believed in the Cherry Tree Principle of Conduct (i.e., "I cannot tell a lie") have an abhorrence for bargaining. We want everything on the table from the word go, as seemingly aboveboard as possible. How much do you want? Put the price up there and let's get it over with. I'll buy it or I won't. Let's not play games. I've got other things to do.

But the Greeks like you to sit down and have a smoke and a cup of coffee over it. They invite the game. They want to *savor* it. It's like sitting in a back room with a cobra. You have to move slowly and carefully.

❉

The morning after Theológos made his offer, Danielle suggested I call our friend Melyá in Athens and ask her for advice.

"Maybe she'd even like to be your partner," she said.

This was such a perfect idea that I immediately started to think of it as my own. Melyá had access to a lot of money. Her ex-husband owned acres of vineyards outside Athens and was one of the most prestigious producers of wine and ouzo in the country. Although he hated giving her any more money than their divorce settlement stipulated, he had been known to help in investments that might permanently get her off his back.

We'd been friends since I first arrived in Greece. Melyá was born and bred into Athenian society, but had somehow managed to escape its habit of endless self-regard. She liked to hang around artists, and I'd met her through my painter friend, Dick. Later, she'd been vital in helping me negotiate my way through the mushrooming complications required to buy our farmhouse. To circumvent the law prohibiting foreigners from owning property on Greece's borders, which is where Patmos is, she had allowed us to use her name on the deed for the house and, in the process, had even purchased a place for herself and her sons from the same family.

A tiny, attractive, vivacious blonde in her forties, she rarely put on makeup and eschewed the fancy Jeeps her sons brought to Patmos, preferring to putter around the island on the kind of cheap motorbike that the Patmians used.

Over the years Melyá and I had indulged in minor fantasies about opening a restaurant or bar together somewhere on the island. Both of us were wont to spend excessive portions of every day planning, purchasing ingredients for, and preparing our evening meals, and such a collaboration would be heaven-sent. She was an acknowledged doyenne on the island and would be able to deal with Theológos on levels I couldn't even begin to imagine, much less fathom.

When I told her about Theológos's offer, and suggested we become partners, Melyá was delighted.

"Oh, *Thomáki*, this will be fabulous! You can cook your wonderful dishes, and we can both be hosts and have wonderful parties, and music and dancing! I can bring people from Athens, and there are our friends from London and Paris and Switzerland and Munich and Vienna! We will be famous and we will make *lots* of money, I guarantee you! *Thomáki*, thank you! I *kiss* you! And Danielle and the children, too!"

I said that I would call Theológos first thing the following morning and close a deal for the two of us to take his tavérna.

"Okay, Thomá," she said. "But be careful. He is very *ponirós*, cunning, like a snake. You want me to call him?"

"No, no. I will do it."

"Okay. If you say so . . ."

※

The next day, I telephoned Theológos, who barely hesitated when I suggested including Melyá in on the deal.

"No," he said, flat out. "I will not rent my tavérna to Melyá."

He wouldn't tell me why. He just said she would not be a good person to rent to. All kinds of implications hung in the air, primarily that she was a woman, and second, rich, a silly dilettante, and third, a *xéni*, a foreigner, from Athens. But he didn't say these things. He left them to my imagination.

I replied that Melyá was my friend, that I trusted and needed her.

"Okay," said Theológos. "Then the two of you find yourself another place to rent, not mine."

The icy inflexibility of his stand was startling. He and Melyá and I had spent innumerable afternoons and evenings over the years sitting at a table in his place laughing and drinking together, she the Athenian society woman, he the Livádi peasant, me the American writer, bonding in the luminous freedom of the Aegean Islands, the great leveling Greek light.

There was a pause. I didn't know what to say.

"Listen," offered Theológos finally, "if you don't have enough money, if you need a partner, we can work things out."

"How—?"

"*I* can be your partner."

"But I thought you didn't want—"

"I don't. It's too much, too much work for someone my age."

He was in his late fifties, but didn't look it, being blessed with that ability that some Greek men have of staying much younger-looking than their women.

"But I can do the shopping," he continued. "Take my caïque and even go to Athens, if you want. We won't run out of supplies like the other places—no beer, no wine. You remember."

I did, vividly. The panic that had regularly ensued during the crowded, final weeks of summer had even prompted some of the foreigners, myself among them, to rent caïques to take them to nearby islands in a desperate search for booze. Like Greece, Patmos had never been self-sufficient. The original imperial Byzantine decree granting the monastery the island had described it as "fallen to waste, covered with brambles and thorny scrub, untrodden and so arid as to be totally barren and infertile." Underneath its present-day trappings, even with the new pier now up and functioning, Patmos was still the same.

During the Nazi occupation, when the island was cut off from outside supplies for almost two years, many Patmians had starved to death, while those who survived subsisted for the most part on animal food and various forms of *hórta* (page 236), the often bitter wild greens that are such a specialty item on today's menus. The experience was burned into the collective Patmian soul as *ee megáli peéna*, the great hunger, and the way in which some of the survivors still husbanded every resource, down to the skimpiest piece of string, was painful and embarrassing for an outsider to watch.

"But we'll have all we need," Theológos continued, "because I'll bring our supplies from the mainland myself. All you have to do is work in the tavérna with Démetra and my sons. They can help you cook and serve. And you give me half the rent— a hundred fifty thousand drachmas. Okay?"

It was amazing how quickly he had come up with this solution. Almost as though he had had it at the ready even before his initial suggestion that I rent it on my own.

Nevertheless, this was not an easy decision for me to make. What would I tell Melyá? On the other hand, I was by now deep into the idea of the tavérna, already there in the kitchen with the Cuisinart food processor I planned to buy, slicing paper-thin cucumbers for the Chinese chicken dish I had in mind. To give that up now as a matter of principle so as not to disappoint Melyá was too much to ask. But she was, after all, a friend. Certainly, she would understand.

Melyá's response was even icier than Theológos's inflexibility. She felt that I had betrayed her. I tried to explain how much I needed this opportunity, and how adamant Theológos had been about not wanting her as a partner. "I couldn't budge him," I said. "I think he's afraid of you."

"For sure."

"I'm sorry," I said, "but I just can't give this up."

There was a long pause.

"Okay, *Thomáki*," she finally answered, her voice softening a bit. "But be careful. Remember what they say about Greeks bringing gifts."

"You and Danielle," I replied, "are a pair of Cassandras."

"It was Laocoön," she answered, "who said that about Greeks bearing gifts. But never mind; Cassandra warned them, too. The point is, Thomá, nobody believed either one."

"I'll remember your warning."

"I hope so."

The Greeks have a deep and ancient distrust of one another that was solidified during their dog-eat-dog scramble to survive the Ottoman occupation. It is a kind of prison mentality, one in which only their closest friends and family are considered trustworthy—and, in a pinch, maybe not even them. In addition, the one true thing that the Greeks have learned about the past is that they are almost certainly condemned to repeat it. The Trojan War, for example, has been raising its ugly head nigh on continuously since the second millennium B.C. Its latest manifestation was in Kosovo, where Greek support of the Serbs surprised only those who didn't realize that the real battle, as far as the Greeks were concerned, was to keep Islam and the Turks (formerly the Trojans) from opening a flank in Europe.

Thus, paranoia is a survival skill well honed over the centuries, and it is the Greek habit of mind to discern portents and intrigues in the most innocent acts, with doom, brought about by fate, international conspiracies, and/or the barbarians from the East, forever imminent.

For these reasons, I would never be able to fully convince Melyá that I had not been intriguing with *O Ladós* behind her back and that dire consequences would result.

On the other hand, I was determined not to let these suspicions drag me down before I even got started.

So, although I dutifully kept in mind exactly what Cassandra and Laocoön had to say about Greeks bearing gifts, I couldn't forget the wonderful, crazy times I'd had with Theológos at The Beautiful Helen over the past nine years.

Foremost was that feast day party at which Danielle and I had finally come together after a summer of keeping a wary distance from one another. Since then, Theológos had taken every opportunity to proudly remind everyone of his role in the affair, as though just because he owned the place where our love affair had begun for everyone to see, he had all but been the *koumbáros*, "best man," at our wedding.

Then there was the yearly pig we had slaughtered and shared in October. Not only had this act ritually consecrated (with actual blood) the bond that was developing between us, but it had allowed me to finally re-create, in Livádi, the special Spaghetti alla Carbonara recipe (page 214) that I had been boasting about to Danielle since the beginning of our relationship. Those of you who are cooks will understand how meaningful this was. Particularly as it involved a promise made to the woman I loved.

Theológos's Pig

If cooking is a form of foreplay (and that's the way it's always seemed to me), then the meal I would invariably use as my opening move in a new relationship was Spaghetti alla Carbonara, whose pungent, slippery-smooth richness makes it— along with canned lychee nuts—just about the sexiest dish around.

At least that's the way it'd been back in America, where everything I needed was right at hand. Greece was another story altogether. And this was especially true of Patmos, where years of poverty, lack of water, and a tradition of strict religious observance had left the stores relatively indifferent to what they stocked and how much.

The approach of Lent, for example, led butchers to start emptying their refrigerators shortly after New Year's and, following a muted Carnival celebration, to leave them that way until Easter. Vanishing along with the meat were all other animal by-products—eggs, milk, and cheese—and any seafood that contained blood: all fish but not squid, octopus, shrimp, and (thank you very much!) lobster. Even the freezers were shorn of their stock during the Lenten season. Meanwhile, on Good Friday, many Patmians limited themselves to sipping vinegar, sometimes mixed with cobwebs, so as to better emulate the sufferings of Jesus.

This was not a place to go looking for delicacies.

But even in Athens in those days, ingredients that you and I take for granted, such as butter, bacon, and bouillon cubes, not to mention soy sauce and curry powder, were rarely available.

As a result, efforts to find or invent substitutes could often raise you to great heights of culinary creativity and/or plunge you into the kind of despair usually associated, in the civilized world, with fallen soufflés or the sudden separation of a seemingly immaculate hollandaise sauce.

My version of Spaghetti alla Carbonara was one that I had adapted from variations practiced in the north and south of Italy.

In Rome, the dish is made by combining piping hot pasta with pieces of butter, chopped, sautéed bacon, eggs beaten with freshly ground black pepper, and a generous handful of grated Parmesan. In Harry's Bar in Milan, heavy cream is substituted for the egg whites, an inclusion that is looked upon by Italian purists as an act of cowardice since it makes scrambling the eggs by mistake almost impossible. But it also gives the dish the same voluptuous texture that is found in the butter-and-cream coating of Fettucini Alfredo. Nevertheless, the Milan variation is a bit heavy, and so my version was a judicious combination of both of the above, substituting cream for only half the egg whites.

Because of the paucity of good grazing lands throughout Greece, heavy cream was nonexistent and fresh milk almost impossible to find. Nor was there such a thing as Greek bacon.

Evaporated milk turned out to be an acceptable (and finally, preferable) substitute for the cream, as it thickens slightly when cooked, but finding the right bacon looked to be an insurmountable problem. The European variety, which was then occasionally available, came out of the can encased in fat as thick as axle grease, was reduced to almost nothing in the frying pan, and had all the flavor impact of lard.

Just as I was despairing of ever reproducing the pungent smokiness I had experienced in Rome and Milan and duplicated in my Manhattan apartment with American bacon, Theológos asked me if I'd like to buy half his yearly pig.

"Pig?" I said.

"Yes," he replied, "the one I have in my field. You know, along the donkey path?"

I recalled occasionally hearing something snort behind a wall as I passed on my way down to the beach.

"Alive?" I inquired.

He smiled. "At the moment."

By this time, Danielle and I had splurged on a refrigerator complete with a reasonably large freezer, and the idea of having half a pig's worth of pork to make chops and sausages with was highly tempting. I was also thrilled at the honor of being asked. This sharing and rendering of a pig was a real crossing of the threshold into Greek life, particularly Greek island life, at its most basic, not to say primitive, level.

"We bring it down to the beach and slaughter it," Theológos continued. "You take half, I take half. What do you say?"

I had a problem, however, with blood.

Several years before, I had had it drawn for a physical and moments later fainted on the spot. I explained the incident to Theológos and also told him about how things in America are so well packaged you hardly ever have to think about their once having been alive. Then, just in case he wasn't getting my point, I also recounted the squeamishness I had experienced while working as an orderly in a New Haven hospital. I had been preparing for a premed degree, but the operations I had seen and the corpses I had trolleyed down to the basement morgue ultimately persuaded me to switch my major to English literature, much to my father's deep disappointment.

In the end, Theológos agreed to slaughter the pig himself and to take the head and heart as part of the deal for doing this.

I stayed away from the beach until it was all over, and then came down in the early evening to take my portions back to the house. Theológos and Eléni and the children were standing behind the kitchen table when I arrived, grinning proudly at what they had prepared for me. Blood was everywhere, on the floor and all over the chopping block table, glistening in the bright fluorescent light that poured down on the area. Lying across the table was my entire half of the pig, still recognizable as this animal that had been sacrificed, unhonored, for me to eat.

The expression on my face must have told all, because Eléni immediately took pity on me and helped cut the carcass into more manageable and anonymous pieces while Theológos sat back and had an ouzo. I put the pieces into plastic bags, and then into canvas sacks, which I hung over my shoulders for the walk back to our house. Theológos toasted me, and Eléni smiled with her gentle brown eyes as I trudged out into the gathering dark, waving aside as theirs my share in the cloven hooves.

That evening, as I prepared to salt, render, mince, freeze, and otherwise put up my booty for the winter, I was ecstatic to find, in my trusty, splattered copy of *The Joy of Cooking*, not only a section on smoke cookery, but a diagram of how to do it. Two days later, after nearly asphyxiating us all, I removed my first efforts from a smoking device jury-rigged out of an olive oil tin in the kitchen chimney and, shortly afterward, experienced the indescribable pleasure of tasting my very own home-made piece of bacon.

It was with this that I finally completed the odyssey I had begun the year before in my attempt to impress Danielle with my expertise at Spaghetti alla Carbonara.

Was it as good as the one I had made in New York? Not really. But as Constantine Cavafy, the great Alexandrian-Greek poet, says in *Ithaca*, his famous piece about another odyssey, the true satisfaction lay in the experiences I had in getting there. Anyway, by that time, Danielle was already, if not exactly mine, at least in my arms and bed.

But to get back to Theológos.

He might have been cunning and wily, as Melyá said, like a snake, and as oily as *O Ladós,* but I knew that if you got past that and appealed to the goodness in him, a whole other person appeared—gruff but expansive, a bear, sometimes a Zorba and at other times a little boy just looking for approval and affection.

I also remembered his once warning me, when I was in the laborious process of buying our farmhouse, not to be so trusting, particularly around Greeks, who would cheat you as soon as look at you.

"Oh?" I said. "But what about you? You're a Greek."

"Me, you can trust," he said, puffing out his chest. Then he wagged his finger in my face. "But nobody else."

How could I not believe in a man like this?

Finally, I was absolutely certain that being an American, from a country that he had visited and so admired, would make me proof against the kinds of tricks he might try on others.

So, I thought, let everyone else—the cynical French and suspicious Greeks—be wary of Theológos. I was not only going to prove them wrong about his character and potential, but the two of us were going to make more than a tidy little sum in the process.

Nine years before, at the age of thirty-three, I had come to Greece with very little money and an unfinished novel. Since then I had lived what most people think is an impossible dream.

I wasn't even going to bother to bargain about the rental price of The Beautiful Helen. And although there was no little voice urging me on this time as it had in my search for a house in Livádi, I knew it was the right thing to do. It had to be.

A final affirmation, a sign, came a few days later when Theológos telephoned to say he had not only found us a house for the summer, but the very one, the house on the hill, that had called out to me on my initial visit to the valley of Livádi so many years before.

We were truly going back to the beautiful beginning of it all, the Golden Age.

The House on the Hill

Back then, at the end of that first day on Patmos, I had been unable to get the house on the hill out of my mind, even though both Theológos and Evripídes had assured me that it was not for rent. So the following morning I got Evripídes to drive me once more out to Livádi.

We stopped on the road halfway down to the beach, directly across from the house. As the crow flies, the distance between it and the road was about a hundred yards. But in between were various fields, a dry riverbed, and numerous stone walls. Evripídes suggested that the easiest way to get there was to go down to the beach and walk up the riverbed. But I didn't want to encounter Theológos and have to explain my actions after he had already told me that the house was not for rent.

Evripídes shrugged and pointed out a cluster of farmhouses just below "my" house on the bluff. These, he said, belonged to the parents of the woman who had inherited it as her dowry. They would be able to tell me what I needed to know. He then smiled, wished me luck, and headed down the hill to turn the *aeropláno* back on course for Skála.

Getting to the house or anywhere near it did not prove to be as easy as it looked from the road. The problem was the stone walls in between, none of which provided an easy entrance from one field to another.

Some of the walls were chest-high and topped with brier or thistles, the latter as sharp as razor wire. In addition, the stones were simply piled one on top of the other, so that when you tried to climb them, they would shift and cause you to reach out for something not stone, like the thistles, for balance. Openings and crossovers may have existed but most were almost imperceptible, and finding my way through and around the walls' serpentine coilings began to seem hopeless. I clambered, stumbled, cursed, sweated, bled, and yelped and saw no one anywhere in sight to ask for guidance.

Finally I reached a steep drop into the thickly bouldered riverbed and was able to make my way down into it by hanging on to the branch of a fig tree spread out over the bed, where it joined trees from the other side to make a wonderfully cool tunnel below. I followed this until I found a path that crossed the riverbed. This, blessedly, took me the rest of the way to the bluff.

Chickens scattered as I approached, and a mule swished its tail in the opening of a stone hut. Next to it, turkeys gobbled inside an enclosure of rusty chicken wire. Wafting across the path came the heavy sweet smell of straw and cattle droppings, and I looked to my left to see a pair of cows chewing their cuds, a cloud of gnats buzzing around their backs. Above them, on top of the rock that formed one side of their yard, was the house I had set my heart on, its two front windows glinting in the sun.

Set among the windows and opening onto the house's terrace were two doors painted a rich ocher trimmed in brown. At the far end of the terrace, there was a small room, clearly an outhouse, its tiny side window facing the sea. A low wall ran along the front of the terrace and iron pipes set into it supported a skeletal wooden trellis wound with the barely visible pale green tendrils of a grapevine. From where I stood, a steep thirty-degree path zigzagged up the rock face to the terrace steps. Opposite this, slightly above me and to my right, was another house, which I imagined to be that of the farmer. As I looked, a woman emerged from its shadowy interior, the morning sun gleaming in the strands of her pulled-back, perfectly white hair.

She looked to be in her sixties but was certainly younger. In places as remote as these, Greek women and men start to age rapidly once into their twenties. A limited diet, lots of exposure to the sun and wind, and virtually nonexistent dental care cause them to lose their teeth at any early age, while their skin becomes permanently browned and creased. The woman's face was webbed with wrinkles and her slightly sunken cheeks bespoke of molars missing from both sides. Her eyes were the most beautiful pale blue I had ever seen, like a baby's, and her smile simply bathed you with kindness.

She asked if I wanted anything.

In my extremely rudimentary Greek, I pointed to the house above us and said I wanted to know if it was for rent.

The tenor of blue in her eyes shifted ever so slightly. "You have to speak my husband," she said and called out, with a sharpness that startled the animals, "Stélios!"

Stélios appeared, a stocky, brown-haired, thickly mustached man with heavily muscled forearms who looked, with his straw hat cocked back on his head, about ten years younger than his wife. He took in my appearance—tousled blond hair, Levi's, and tourist sandals—and nodded with a certain gruff reserve, although there was a sparkle of curiosity in his hazel eyes.

This sparkle turned into a smile when he heard me attempt Greek, and he listened carefully as I tried to explain how I had seen his house from the beach and liked it and was a writer and needed a place to stay through the summer so I could finish my novel.

When I finished, he said, "*Vevávos,* of course. Why not? We can rent it to you."

He then explained that their daughter, who usually came for the summer, had just called to say she was pregnant and would stay in Athens. So—just as my little voice had promised—there was no problem!

He and his wife, whose name was Varvára, then took me up to the house, opening one of the doors with a long iron key.

We stepped into a narrow kitchen whose single window on the left overlooked the barnyard below. The kitchen walls were whitewashed and the woodwork painted a slightly faded turquoise green. There was no running water, just a fauceted plastic container attached to the open shutter on one side of the window. A single lightbulb hung in the center of a beamed ceiling. In the wall opposite the door a two-burner butane stove sat in a waist-high fireplace, whose opening was arched in stone. A second, smaller opening behind it led to a huge domed oven, its interior visible as the morning sunlight bounced up into it off the wooden floorboards. I would have rented the house for that cooking area alone.

A door to the right led to the middle room. It was slightly narrower than the kitchen and had a shelved open cupboard set into one wall with a table beneath it. The window looked out the front of the house over the terrace to the plain below and the sea beyond. A perfect place for writing.

Through another door was the largest room in the house, the bedroom-living room. Its two windows, one facing the front, the other the far side of the house, were both shuttered, but in the shadows of the far corner, I could make out an ornate, four-postered wrought-iron double bed, a medallion in its headboard delicately painted with a bouquet of pastel-colored flowers.

The rent, Stélios announced, puffing up his chest, was five hundred drachmas a month. Half of what Theológos had asked for a room. About sixteen dollars. It was almost embarrassing. I didn't even think of bargaining. How could you imagine lowering a price as low as that?

On the terrace was an unglazed clay amphora, its top bosoming outward from the base. In its narrow neck, there were two looped handles just large enough to crook a finger in. Stélios did this and deftly hoisted it to his shoulder, the bulge preventing it from slipping backward. He grinned. *"Neró,"* he said.

I grinned in return, nodding idiotically.

Varvára tapped me on the shoulder and pointed down the hill, beyond her and Stélios's house to a field about fifty yards away. In the middle of the field was a circular concrete area that was the unmistakable cap of a well. She smiled. *"Neró,"* she said.

"Ah!" I replied. "Water!"

That would be the source of my water. The amphora held about three gallons and I would have to haul it up daily to drink, wash dishes and clothes in, and use for the toilet. In the romantic cloud I was then inhabiting, this seemed as perfect as it could be, healthy, invigorating, calorie-consuming. Two years later, however, when Danielle and I returned from an Athens maternity clinic with Sara and her diapers in our arms, the picture would not seem quite as rosy.

Stélios and Varvára invited me down to their terrace to conclude our arrangement with a ritual cup of Greek coffee and a tiny dish of preserved quince that Varvára herself had put up. The syrup in which it was encased was unbearably sweet, but the taste of quince itself slightly smoky and wonderfully exotic. The Greeks make these preserves in several varieties—pear, peach, cherry, watermelon, fig, and even eggplant. Collectively, they are called spoon sweets, *gleeká tou koutalyú*, because they are eaten with a spoon, not spread with a knife on bread. Often, they are accompanied by an equally unbearably sweet liqueur, such as mint or banana. Fortunately, Varvára handed me a glass of water. "Our" water. It was cool and clear and as delicious as a taste of spring air.

We wrote our agreement down on a piece of lined notebook paper, and I grandly left a deposit of two months' rent in advance—thirty-two dollars—saying that I would return to Mykonos to get my books and papers and be back in a few days.

Stélios showed me how to get down to the beach, setting me off on a narrow dirt path between two waist-high stone walls that wound across the riverbed and then continued its separate serpentine way to the shore, ending exactly at the side of The Beautiful Helen. On the way, I passed fields green with late winter plantings of tomatoes, zucchini, eggplant, and onions. Occasionally, a lone donkey would bray at me, and from behind a wall of planted green bamboo came the nervous snort of a mule, startled by my sudden, foreign passing.

When I rounded the corner of the tavérna, eager to lord my triumph over Theológos, the caïque that he had been painting the previous day was nowhere in sight.

I peered through the cloudy Plexiglas windows of the tavérna.

Theodóra, the daughter, was sweeping up. She came and opened the door, motioning me in. I asked for her father. He had gone to the port with her brothers in the caïque.

A voice called out from the kitchen wishing me good morning.

"Kaliméra!"

From behind the wall came Eléni, Theológos's wife. She was a wiry little woman in her thirties, with sparkling brown eyes and lustrous raven-black hair. She was wiping her hands on her apron, and her body, as she stood between me and the cooking area, had a firmness of stance that told you that this kitchen was definitely her domain.

I introduced myself and related the good news about the house I'd found. They professed delight. Then Eléni asked how much the rent was. I told her. She shook her head sadly.

"Too much!"

"Too much?!"

"Neró?" she asked, turning her hand upward, palm empty.

I later learned that in Greece hers was a common reaction to almost any figure anybody ever quoted about anything. The price was never right, the buyer always cheated. Which is why no one in the country, with the exception of naïve foreigners like myself, ever tells anyone what they paid for something. They instead imply with winks, nudges, and a satisfied smile that they themselves badly bamboozled the seller.

But never mind. At that moment, St. John himself would

not have felt more blessed than I, as I sat outside *Ee Oráya Eléni* in the midday sun, attended to by Eléni and Theodóra, and had the first glorious lunch of what I mistakenly planned to be just a single lovely summer on Patmos, spent in the splendid isolation of my rough stone house on the hill. . . .

Now, nearly a decade later, I would be returning there to live in that same house as the proprietor of The Beautiful Helen. It seemed to me that things couldn't have been more perfect, the circle more complete.

And what made the prospect even better was the fact that during the interval, using money from the two years of rent I had paid, Stélios had built a cistern in front of the house. We would have running water.

Givers and Takers

"When can you give me the money?"

This was not quite the response I had been expecting when I told Theológos that I would definitely accept his offer of a partnership. I don't know exactly what I had envisaged—something akin to the breaking of a bottle of champagne on the bow of The Beautiful Helen, I suppose—but certainly nothing so blunt as his immediate request for cash. Like most Americans, I am uncomfortable not only with bargaining but with most of the other cold, hard facts of business dealings. Instead, I prefer my naked self-interest to be clothed in some higher purpose, such as family or the good of society as a whole.

Greeks, on the other hand, may be among the very best in charm and camaraderie in leading up to a deal, but once an agreement is reached, their approach quickly zeros in on the basics. With Theológos's abrupt request to see the money, I was immediately made aware of a subtle but seismic shift in the ground of our relationship. In his eyes, I was now a different person. I had crossed the line between the tourists and the Greeks. I was no longer a giver; I was a taker.

Later I would find out that Theológos's perception would be shared by almost everyone else on Patmos, that as soon as my new status became known, my relationships with both my Greek and my foreign friends would undergo a similar, and initially almost imperceptible, transformation. It was as gradual as the fading of daylight in the late autumn, when suddenly it is dark at 5 P.M., and you don't know how it happened.

But for the time being, I would sense this change only in Theológos. And even then, I brushed it aside as a figment of my overly dramatic imagination.

※

I told Theológos that it would probably take a while to have the money transferred from my bank account in Switzerland and promised that I would send it as soon as it arrived.

"No," he said. "I'll come and get it."

"Here? To Crete?!"

It was an arduous journey—twelve hours by ship from Patmos to Piraeus, then another nine from Piraeus to Iráklion, Crete's largest port, and then one and a quarter hours by bus to Rethymnon. And if you did it as Theológos probably would, in third class, sitting up all the way, it was torturous.

He claimed he didn't mind, saying that he didn't trust sending such a large sum through the mail or the banks or telegraph office.

He was right. I had often had money go mysteriously astray for a week or longer when sent through the usual channels within Greece. Eventually, I came to the conclusion that this was not accidental. The longer the banks and telegraph systems kept the money, the more interest they could make. This would come to a considerable sum if all the amounts sent by cable and bank wire in Greece were deposited in an interest-bearing government account for just a single extra day, not to mention a week. As for the postal system, well, it had recently taken a month for a letter of mine to travel from Crete to Patmos, and you often heard documented stories of underpaid postal workers simply tossing entire bags of mail into the garbage because they couldn't be bothered with them.

Finally, the Greeks considered personal checks so blatant a device for cheating, for acquiring something without actually paying for it (and maybe never doing so), that they—checks—were beneath contempt and rarely, if ever, accepted in even the largest financial transactions.

Thus, no matter how great the sum, it was always carried in briefcases or paper bags filled with cash on the line. And in those days, when the largest bill was only one thousand drachmas, this could prove to be not only unwieldy but scary. Greek newspapers had stories almost daily about fortunes being snatched from the grasp of pedestrians by thieves whizzing by on motorbikes.

Above all, however, Theológos didn't want any official documentation of our deal, nothing that the tax authorities might be able to trace back to him. Such practices were the norm in Greece. Everybody cheated the government, and only a fool was honest about his income.

This behavior was justified on two levels. First, government officials were uniformly dishonest and lined their pockets at every opportunity. They also filled cushy civil servant positions with their friends and relatives, who paid them a percentage for the privilege of collecting a salary and pension in a job at which they didn't have to work. So why should you, an ordinary citizen, be left holding the bag? Second, since the authorities expected everyone to lie about their income, they automatically taxed you for much more than you reported anyway. Therefore, cheating was also a justified attempt to right the wrong of being arbitrarily overtaxed in the first place.

So I agreed with Theológos to conduct the transfer of funds in person as soon as the money arrived from Switzerland.

✳

I then telephoned Melyá to break the news, hoping I could lay her recent suspicions to rest by being relentlessly aboveboard about the remainder of my dealings with Theológos. She and I were not only friends but, for a brief wild period when I first hit Mykonos, had been lovers. Afterward, upon the birth of Danielle's and my first child, Melyá had become almost a part of the family, virtually a godmother for both children. It now seemed absurd that something as silly as this obvious misunderstanding could permanently come between us.

But Melyá didn't quite see it that way.

"Thomá," she said, "first, you ask me to be your partner, and then you make an arrangement with Theológos behind my back. Now you want us to be friends?! How stupid do you think I am? What are you—CIA?"

"Melyá—"

She hung up.

The Cretan Connection

It was strange to encounter him in a city, sitting in our living room in Rethymnon, this man who normally walked around with his pants legs rolled up and plastic flip-flops on his feet. Now he seemed a fish out of water, dressed like a schoolboy in a rumpled blue suit with a much washed, badly ironed white shirt buttoned at the collar. His shoes were black and recently polished, and his tan socks had little multicolored diamond patterns on them. A dark brown fedora rested on his lap.

The picture had something of the suppliant about it, of a working-class man appearing before his betters. But perhaps this was what I was reading into it. Otherwise, Theológos appeared relaxed, familiar, entirely affable. He was also very solicitous toward me, wanting to know my plans for the tavérna and ready to advise and guide me in achieving what I wanted. We were, I kept reminding myself, soon-to-be partners.

Amazingly, Danielle seemed to have entirely dropped her reservations about the deal. She appeared genuinely pleased to see Theológos and eager to discuss how things would be handled in the summer.

Theológos was worried that I might not understand how hard the work would be. I assured him that I did and told him about the restaurant job I had taken in Rethymnon after Matt's birth two summers before. I had not only waited on tables but helped cook the food and prepare the salads. Lunch had been mildly stressful, dinner hell. There had hardly been a moment's respite between the two, and even when there was, fresh dinner dishes had to be made, salads cut, and the detritus of lunch washed away. I had no illusions about the insanity awaiting me on Patmos.

"How many people could you seat?" Theológos asked.

"Ten, twelve."

He smiled. On quiet days, there was room at The Beautiful Helen for three times as many, and at the height of the season, when business spread across the road to the beach, four times that.

"You know, I won't be able to help you very much," Theológos reiterated for what seemed like the hundredth time. "I am going to have to take people on tours around the island in my new caïque. Of course, I'll bring them to the tavérna for lunch, but I won't do any serving. You understand that?"

I did, I did. And in a way, I was happy about it. I didn't want to be seen as working for Theológos or really even with him. I wanted to put my stamp on The Beautiful Helen. I wanted people to say, *"Ahs fámeh sto Thomá,"* "Let's eat at Tom's place."

"Of course," said Theológos, "on the fifth of August, the eve of the *paneyíri,* I'll be there."

I glanced at Danielle, again remembering the feast day party when she and I had tried, hand in hand, to walk on water as at least a hundred people stood chanting in a semicircle around us, urging us on.

"You won't be able to do it without me," continued Theológos. "It's crazy, crazy!"

He caught the glance between Danielle and me and grinned like a proud father. "Crazy!"

※

The contract we drew up on a lined sheet of classroom paper stipulated the following:

1. that I was paying Theológos 150,000 drachmas to rent the tavérna from June 15 to September 15;
2. that Theológos and I would split the profits fifty-fifty at the end of the summer;
3. that in the interim, we would both receive a salary of 10,000 drachmas a week (then about 220 dollars), keeping the rest aside for expenses;
4. that I would be the tavérna's cook and host and that Theológos would deal only with purchasing supplies;
5. that Theológos's two sons, Lámbros and Sávas, would work in various capacities for a salary of 45 dollars a week;
6. and that Démetra, the woman he had recently brought into the tavérna as a cook and cleaning lady, would continue on in that capacity for 90 dollars a week.

Theológos said that Stélios and Varvára were eagerly awaiting our return to their little house on the hill and had already
found both an extra bed for Sara and a crib for Matt. He
looked at Danielle, waiting for an expression of thanks.
Instead, she said, "What about a work permit?"

I've noticed that women frequently do this. They wait until
you've made all kinds of plans and then, at the last minute, just
as you're in the car and ready to go, they say, "Wait! What
about—?"

"Huh?" I replied.

"I just thought," said Danielle, "won't you need some kind of
permit?"

I turned to Theológos. He, too, seemed momentarily at a
loss. Actually, this possible difficulty had already occurred to
me, but since no one had brought it up, I'd brushed it aside, figuring, I suppose, that if it wasn't mentioned, it somehow
wouldn't exist. But now the cat was out of the bag. When you
live in a foreign country as long as I had, particularly in a place
as tiny as Patmos, you start to feel you belong there, and that
you have the same rights as its citizens. But of course this isn't
true. Ever. Not even if you're an American.

Theológos barely batted an eyelash.

"No problem," he said. "Everybody knows Thomás. They
won't bother us."

"You're sure?" Danielle asked. "Won't the police . . ."

Theológos smiled at her as if at a little child. "I will tell
them Thomás helps me, like a friend. That's what they want to
hear. Then they will leave us alone."

He was right. The authorities simply needed something,
anything, to justify turning a blind eye. This sort of stuff went
on all the time. I pointed out to Danielle that no one had bothered me the previous summer when I was working in the
restaurant here in Rethymnon.

"Yes," she replied, "but not as a partner."

"It is not problem," said Theológos. "Don't worry."

After a moment, she shrugged, giving in. Much later, she would say to me, "Well, you were ten years older. I thought you knew absolutely everything."

※

Upon the signing of the contract, Theológos and I had a glass of *rakí,* a Cretan schnapps, to celebrate. Then I took him into our kitchen to show him the lunch I was preparing. It was a dish I intended to make at The Beautiful Helen, what I hoped would be an exotic offering of Mexican-American Chili con Carne (page 216).

Theológos stared down at the bubbling, aromatic contents of the pot, then extracted a kidney bean with a spoon.

"You eat this?" he said.

"Certainly. Why?"

"We don't."

"But—they sell the beans in the market!" I said. "Huge sacks of them!"

Theológos smiled. "Of course."

"So?"

"It is food for animals. If human beings eat these, they will get sick."

"Not in America!" I replied, as if this should somehow set a world standard in the matter.

Theológos shrugged. "Well . . ." he said, and dropped the bean back in the pot.

With my hundred and fifty thousand drachmas in thousand-drachma notes bulging in his pockets, he then insisted on taking us out to lunch. We went down to Rethymnon's elegant Venetian harbor and feasted, indoors, on what was for all of us the rare treat of grilled red mullet, *barbúni,* the champagne of

Mediterranean fish. We accompanied it with a crisp winter salad of shredded romaine lettuce and green onion, slices of feta cheese, and much white Cretan wine from Iráklion. By the time we'd finished, the windows of the tavérna had fogged over from the heat of our appetites, and we fell back into cups of strong Greek coffee, satiated and very satisfied—at least Theológos and I were—with ourselves.

An hour or so later, he headed back to Iráklion for business, after which he would spend the night with relatives and, the following evening, embark on his long journey back to Patmos.

❋

I was feeling good about everything. The fact that we had come from Patmos to live on Crete, and that Theológos, who is descended from Cretans, had traveled here to close the deal, seemed particularly propitious.

The relationship between Crete and Patmos had lasted nearly nine hundred years and had been extremely fruitful. Not only had Cretan laborers endured enormous hardships to build the monastery, but they had also forced Christódoulos, the austere Byzantine monk who brought them there for that purpose, to rescind his edict forever "defending" what he called his "workshop of virtue" against the presence of women. Thus was born the first secular community on Patmos. Later, the innate shrewdness of the Cretans would help create the merchant fleet that had brought such wealth to the island.

This was Theológos's heritage, and the blond mop of his one towheaded son, Lámbros, left no doubt about its legitimacy. He had a genetic connection not just to Crete but specifically to that proudly independent tribe of Sfákians who still hide themselves away among the mountains of its southwestern corner. Many are as blond as their ancestors, the Dorians, invaders of Greece a thousand years before Christ, and most are said to be the wildest brigands on an island renowned for its rugged individualists. But, like all such mountain types, from the Montagnards of Vietnam to the Sicilian Mafia, they are also known to be fiercely loyal to outsiders whom they consider friends.

Theológos, *O Ladós, Patmiótis, Sfakianós*. My new partner.

"So," said Danielle when we returned home from our celebratory feast with Theológos and were standing in the kitchen looking at the untouched pot of chili, "what are you going to do about this?"

"Make it anyway," I answered. "The foreigners will love it!"

The Main Course

Home Again

Out of the thick velvet darkness the lights of Patmos appear, first one and then another and another, not at sea level as you'd expect, but high above you, like stars, as if the island were caught up in some sort of celestial levitation.

Then, just when you're beginning to get your bearings, the lights abruptly vanish, and there is again nothing but darkness. Even when you know why, the effect is still disconcerting. What has happened is that the mountain of Cape Yénoupas, sulfurous lair of the *mágus* that St. John turned to stone, has suddenly come between you and the lights, blotting them out as if they had been swallowed by a black hole.

But as the ship continues its swing around the southern and eastern promontories, the harbor comes into view, and Patmos is at last brought down to earth. Ahead are the bright, welcoming lights of Skála reaching toward you as they stretch shimmering on the surface of the sea. And above, to the left, the stars are revealed to be the street lamps of Hóra, discreetly wreathing the base of the dark and nearly invisible monastery.

We arrived in early June, Danielle and the children and I, about ten days before I was to become a partner in the tavérna. After nearly two years of having been away from the island, I had been impatiently standing on deck for the last half hour, leaning on the railing as if I could get the ship there sooner by willpower alone. When Skála came into view, Danielle joined me with the children. The docking process was excruciatingly slow as the ship put its engines into reverse, dropped anchor, carefully swung around to avoid the lurking underwater rock of Yénoupas, and finally backed toward the pier, lowering its ramp as it went.

I held Sara up at the railing, trying to make her remember landmarks she had seen only a few times in her brief existence and couldn't possibly have recalled. Beside me, Danielle quietly cradled an exhausted Matt, inert as a sack of beans.

It was ten o'clock at night, a Saturday, and on the dock, a sparse crowd of familiar Patmian faces milled about waiting either for goods and relatives to disembark or to board the ship themselves as it continued south to Rhodes. Nearly all of the faces belonged to people we had gotten to know in one way or another over the years, sometimes when we weren't even aware of it. Once, when I was writing a guide to the island, I had trekked to its southern side to have a look at a remote ravine where legend said that St. John had vanquished a man-eating monster. There, perched on the side of the slope leading down into the ravine, in an area so crisscrossed with mountains and hills that there was not another man-made structure for miles in all directions, sat a tiny stone farmhouse with a rock-strewn vegetable garden and jerry-built chicken coop. To get to the ravine, I would have to use the house's entrance path. As I slid down the pebbly surface, a woman I was certain I had never seen before came out, looked me up and down, and delightedly said, "*Thomá! Tee kánis edthó?* What are you doing here? How are the wife and your little daughter? Good?" After that, I never again doubted that absolutely everyone on Patmos knew almost as much about my business as I did myself—with seemingly instantaneous updates. Witness Theológos's awareness of how, when, and to whom I had sold the farmhouse.

For this reason, Melyá would have known we were arriving

that night even though I hadn't spoken to her for five months, not since she'd hung up on me following her still-painful accusation that I had the character, and perhaps credentials, of a CIA agent. In the old days, even if she had not come down to the pier herself, she would have alerted whatever foreign friends of ours were on the island, and there would have been at least one of them waiting to lead us to a round of welcoming drinks at the Arion café, our anointed waterfront rendezvous. Now, the only familiar faces on the pier were Patmians, and they didn't have time for these sorts of late night indulgences. For them, unless they were café and restaurant workers, it was always early to bed, early to rise, particularly in the summer when there was double or triple the usual heavy load of work to be done, and particularly on a Saturday night when the following morning's chores would have to be finished before church.

We spotted Theológos and his sons, waved, and headed down into the hold where I had piled our bags and boxes, many laden with cookbooks and kitchen supplies. I lugged off what I could and then returned with Theológos's sons, Sávas and Lámbros, for the rest as Theológos, ever the boss, stood watch over what I had already brought. The boys and I plowed our way through the two-way traffic of everyone trying to get on and off at once and managed to grapple the rest of my belongings to shore seconds before the ship began its clanking, churning separation from the dock.

Danielle and the children, meanwhile, had been surrounded by Patmians, mostly women, all eager to measure Sara's progress and to see Matt, the new addition to the family. *"Na sas zísi!"* they were saying, which roughly means, May it (the child) live its life for you!

I wanted to go to the Arion to find out who was there, but Danielle and then Theológos quickly closed ranks to veto the idea. She was exhausted, she said, and so were the children. Theológos added that he had to get up early the next morning. It was the Sunday of Pentecost. There would be memorial services for the dead at the church on the hill, and afterward, many in the congregation would be making the season's traditional first trip to the beach, where they would lunch at the tavérna.

In other words, these weren't the good old days any longer, when I could just go off celebrating our arrival with my buddies at the Arion. I was a husband and a father now, of two children no less, and what I was on Patmos for—in case I'd forgotten—was business.

So I dutifully followed Theológos and my wife and children around the harbor to his spanking new caïque, the *Pandóra II*, and loaded everything aboard. Then we chugged out into the darkness, the glittering lights of Skála slowly diminishing in the distance like the final shot of one of those old Eastmancolor travelogues, with the voice-over intoning, "And so we bid farewell . . ."

And in fact, although I wasn't aware of it then, this would be the last time I would see Skála again at night until almost the middle of August.

※

There was no wind, and the boat's powerful engine moved us easily through the smooth, dark water. The *Pandóra II* was definitely several steps up from its predecessor, and I could feel my hundred and fifty thousand drachmas all over it, in the engine, in the solid brass fittings, and in the state-of-the-art two-way radio that sat on a forward shelf inside its spacious cabin. There were bright, flowery, chintz curtains on the portholes, and matching cushions on the side and central benches. In between the two front windows, a small electric light simulating a wick burning in a jar of oil illuminated a brass clock in the shape of ship's wheel, and above it, an icon of St. Nicholas, a copy of one that had washed up ages before on the northern shores of Pat-mos—in that harsh, wind-ravaged headland where Theológos had been born—and was said to possess miraculous properties, particularly for those in peril on the sea.

The old *Pandóra*'s cabin had been able to seat eight maximum; now there was room for at least fifteen and even more on the open deck. Theológos stood to make a bundle ferrying tourists around in the summer. I didn't begrudge him. We were both in it for the money, and in the process, were demonstrating a primary principle of capitalism in action, with my initial investment already rippling outward to *ee poleé*, the many: to Theológos, to his shipbuilder, to the supplier of his accessories, and soon to his sons, who, I was proud to think, would probably be making the first independent money of their lives from the salary I would be paying them.

※

I looked at the boys sitting together on the other side of the cabin talking with Sara, laying on the charm. Sávas, now about fifteen, had his mother's coloring, black hair, limpid brown eyes, long dark lashes, and a flush of red high in his cheeks. Lámbros, a year younger, had the same coloring in his cheeks but the rest of his features, as already noted, were a throwback to his blue-eyed, blond, Dorian ancestors. And whereas Sávas was small-boned and delicate, open-faced Lámbros was already acquiring the stockiness of a soccer player. But both had, for young Greek males, an astonishing gentleness about them, as if their mother were still hovering around somehow, still a mitigating presence in their lives.

When we'd first met, they'd been about Sara's age, but were already hard at work trailing after their father helping him with the seemingly endless series of tasks he daily set for himself. There was the scraping, caulking, and painting of the caïque;

the continual refurbishing of the tavérna as he jerry-built "improvements" on it (some of them, like the cutting down of the huge tamarisk shade tree in its center, tragically misconceived), and the treks to the small plot of land he had back in the valley, where, along with the usual plantings of tomatoes, zucchini, peppers, eggplants, and onions, he kept some chickens, a donkey, and that aforementioned pig he annually bought as a baby and fattened through the summer with slops from the kitchen.

And when they were finished doing these things, the boys would then go to the tavérna to help their mother and their older sister, shy, red-cheeked Theodóra, in the kitchen.

So the occasions when Theológos would leave the island on one of his business trips were ones of great and sudden joy as the boys leapt up to grasp, with their mother's quiet approval, a rare chance to simply be boys. You could always tell when Theológos was setting off on a trip. The first thing you'd see, as soon as the *Pandóra* had turned the headland, would be Sávas and Lámbros stripping off their clothes and racing across the beach to throw their pale white bodies into the sea, clad in only their ragged shorts.

Now they were just about to grow into men. And there they were already taking on the role of big brothers with Sara, keeping her entertained during the slow boat ride out to Livádi.

Sara's Greek was much better than mine, and so were her social skills. She had made many friends on the streets of Rethymnon, and recently I had watched her join them in the leaping over of tiny bonfires lit to celebrate a feast day—of St. Lazarus, I believe—something I would never have been caught dead doing, if you'll pardon the pun.

Sara had hated being torn away from Rethymnon for the summer, but now it seemed she had quickly changed her mind, taking a seat between the boys and animatedly chattering away while squirming, too, with that natural flirtatiousness that even six-year-old girls have in abundance.

Danielle and I caught each other's eye and smiled. This was one problem solved. Meanwhile, Matt was still dead to the world on her lap, the pacifier that he had yet to relinquish, even though he had just passed his second birthday, solidly plugged into his mouth.

The former caïque's engine had rattled and spat like a rapid-fire ack-ack gun; the new one, although considerably quieter, had a resonating thump that still made talking without shouting nearly impossible. So all of us eventually lapsed into silence, giving in to the roll of the sea, the rhythmic pulse of the pistons, and the star-dusted immensity of the nighttime sky. In the stern, Theológos stood with his hand on the tiller, gazing ahead, his silhouette dark against the firmament.

Some twenty minutes later, Livádi hove into view, its farming families already asleep. Except for a few widely dispersed lamps lighting the valley road and pathways, the only illumination came—as usual—from The Beautiful Helen, whose bright fluorescence poured out across the road and onto the beach.

Démetra was on the tiny stone pier to greet us and grab the hawser. She was a hard-muscled, diminutive woman in her mid-forties with pale blue eyes, apple cheeks, and a gold-capped incisor that glinted when she smiled, which was often. Her frizzled, graying brown hair was always tightly done up in a kerchief, as if this were the only way to keep it from bursting out into electric proportions. She was full of a bright vim and vigor, and when she spoke, she barked out her words, slapping you on the back with them. For years she'd been living in a childless marriage with a sad, scrawny, dirt-poor farmer who had a cataract in one eye, and then, one day, she suddenly appeared in the tavérna working for Theológos, and you knew that she and the farmer were finished, even though he'd now and then pass by the tavérna and eventually even came to sit and eat there.

This had only happened a few months before we left the island, so I had still not become accustomed to the possibility, or what I felt was the certainty, that she and Theológos were lovers. Part of my inability to get my mind around this had to do with the sense of loyalty I still felt toward Eléni, who had fed and mothered me through my first summer in the valley and whose name I still applied to the tavérna, as if she were its true heart and soul, its patron saint. But I suspect that a large part of my resistance came from the difficulty I had in picturing Theológos, with his sun-browned arms and pale white body, wrapping tiny, gold-toothed Démetra in a passionate embrace.

I liked Démetra a lot, though. She'd always had a genuinely cheery greeting for us, and tonight was no exception. It was clear that she was very much looking forward to our working together. So was I. I knew that she would be indefatigable both in keeping the tavérna clean and in cooking the standard Greek fare that I didn't want to bother with. I also knew that she would do exactly as I wished, without needing to inject her own opinions—a rare experience for me, I might add, in the nine years I had lived with Danielle's irrepressible Gallic contentiousness, which was always ready for a good difference of opinion, even if all you said was that it looked to be a nice day.

We went up to The Beautiful Helen to leave my boxes of kitchen paraphernalia. As we entered, my warm recollections of its cozy interior were instantly dispelled in the harsh glare of the overhead neons. What had seemed cozy in my mind's eye was now simply crowded and tawdry, piled with chairs and tables and cheap plastic crates with beer, soft drink, and wine bottles. The whitewash on the upper half of the walls was cracked and stained from the winter humidity, and on the lower half, Theológos, for reasons known only to him, had applied a shade of a pale green usually seen, in the Western world anyway, in hospital operating rooms.

Separating the main room from the kitchen were two glass-fronted display cases, one that I remembered from before, sprayed with several coats of yellowing refrigerator paint that could not hide the rust, the other brand new, its burnished stainless steel radiant in the bright neon lights. In season, they would be cornucopias bursting with food and drink; now, their skimpy offerings sat lonely and separated on the inside racks like the sad supplies of a bachelor's refrigerator.

I stood there, taking it all in as it really was and not as I had wanted it to be, and instantly abandoned the fantasies I had had about fixing things up. What had I been thinking of? The only way there could be improvements here would be to raze the entire structure to the ground and start all over again.

I looked at Danielle. She, too, had just finished looking things over and was turning to Theológos, smiling. "*Oráyo!*" she said, indicating the hospital-green paint and the new display case. "Beautiful!"

I wondered, briefly, if there was something wrong with me.

※

After we had put my boxes in the back, we loaded Theológos's donkey with our personal belongings and, accompanied by the boys, headed once again into the darkness, this time up the narrow, serpentine path that led alongside and through the dry riverbed to our old house on the hill.

The moon was rising behind us, but I think I could have made the journey with my eyes closed. As I took my turn carrying our now restless son, a thousand-and-one-nights of memories came flooding back to me, not so much in my mind's eye as through the outward senses—the smells of drying thyme and oregano and the pungent odor of animal droppings and manure-mixed earth; the feel of powdery dirt of the path between my toes and the soft night breezes brushing my skin; and the rhythmic humming of crickets and frogs from the tiny marsh that lay on one side of the valley, counterpointed by the clops and creaks of Theológos's donkey and the occasional clink of the bell of an animal alerted to our approach. All of these in all of those seasons in the valley had become so imprinted on my senses that now they seemed to be not simply around my body but flowing through it, embracing me.

Varvára and Stélios's house was dark. They always awoke with the animals at 3 or 4 A.M. and so were usually asleep by nine. We quietly carried our things up the rocky incline to our house, and then the boys wished us good night and left.

The rooms were almost exactly as they had been when we'd left four years before to move into our finally renovated farmhouse across the way. But now, there was running water in the kitchen and toilet, stored in a large concrete cistern built on to the front of the terrace and pumped to a small tank on the roof.

In the middle room, my former writing room, they had placed a cot for Sara and, much to our surprise and delight, for Matt, the same portable bed we had bought for Sara when she was his age. We had left it for Varvára and Stélios's grandchildren and now it was coming back to us.

In our room, a new double bed with a headboard of varnished veneer sat in place of the wrought-iron, four-postered one that had been there when I first arrived. The original, with its bouquet of flowers hand-painted on a medallion in the center of the headboard, was now in Rethymnon. When we had moved to our farmhouse, we had begged Varvára and Stélios to sell it to us, this romantic trysting spot where we had first made love and had conceived Sara. They consulted their daughter in Athens. Thankfully, she had no emotional connection whatsoever to the bed. When Varvára and Stélios gave us the good news, they watched our reaction while leaning their bodies against each other like lovebirds on a branch, happily grinning.

We put the children to bed, turned off the lights, and got into bed ourselves, huddling together beneath sheets whose chilly, rough cotton had certainly not been warmed by human contact since the previous summer. Right then, it occurred to me that with only a thin, glass-paneled pair of imperfectly closing doors between our room and the children's, the chances of making love with any sense of freedom or abandon for the next three months were almost nil.

I communicated this to Danielle, who tried to console me. "You know how deeply they sleep. And they'll be very tired, playing on the beach all day."

"Um," I replied.

"What else can we do?"

"I don't know."

I listened for a long minute. Not a sound was coming from their room. We were sleeping, as always, in the nude, and Danielle's skin was still as silky as it had been all those years before. I turned a little toward her.

"Do you think they're asleep now?" I asked.

"Tom!"

※

I may have slept. I must have, because several hours certainly passed. But it seemed as if my brain had never stopped teeming with shoals of anxieties, thrashing about, leaping up to grab my attention, and then splashing down into the depths to be immediately replaced by others even worse.

What was I doing, risking so much of our capital on that tawdry tavérna out here in the Greek equivalent of the Ozarks? And what qualified me for this? It wasn't going to be like cooking at home for four, eight, or even ten people. With luck we would have fifty or more a night, a hundred or two hundred a day. And only a small portion of them would be friends. But even with the latter, it wouldn't be like guests coming over for dinner. At home, I had been able to ensure against failure by using my father's old trick of plying your company with so much alcohol beforehand that by they time they sat down, sloshed and ravenous, canned spaghetti would have tasted good. And there was always the politeness factor. Even if dinner was bad, nobody would come right out and say so.

Now, not only would a large number of these people, particularly the Greeks, hardly be drinking at all but every one of them, including my friends, would be paying. And all the politeness would have to be coming from me.

Did I really know how to cook? I mean, really? Just because I could shine with a few specialties like Spaghetti alla Carbonara and Chinese Chicken with Cucumbers and had had a subscription to *Gourmet* magazine for ten years? Or because I knew the difference between tournedos Rossini and tournedos Chasseur, between chalupas and chapatis, and a 1958 and 1959 Château Lafite Rothschild? Who would care? It was just window dressing.

And who could guarantee anyone would show up, particularly now that I had alienated Melyá? Greeks were capable of spreading wild rumors about others, particularly foreigners. In Rethymnon, I had been told by friends that a young Cretan, a teenager, who had hung around Socrátes's restaurant while I was there, was not only telling everyone that I was a spy but that he intended to shoot me. I immediately announced I was going to the police. My friends stopped me. "Don't worry," they said. "He's taken care of." Two days later, he was drafted and disappeared into the wilds of northern Greece to patrol the border with Albania. How this happened, I don't know. But

Melyá was a high-class Athenian Greek and much subtler. Bullets weren't her style. There were a lot of other ways she could take you down, and you wouldn't even know it. Nor would anybody else.

But it was past 3 A.M., the dark night of the soul, and I was getting paranoid. "Beware of wandering into your head alone," my painter friend Dick had once warned me. "It's a dangerous neighborhood!"

Danielle, the only person available to take along with me on this walk on the wild side, was sound asleep, purring like a kitten, and anyway, being a guy, I felt compelled to deal with these anxieties on my own. So to clear my head, I slipped out of bed and crept onto the terrace to have one of those cigarettes that I have now long since given up.

The silence was profound. The crickets and frogs had stopped for the night, and the roosters and donkeys hadn't yet awoken. The valley and sea were a ghostly silver under the moonlight, and there was a silence behind the silence that was immense, holy, sovereign, like the voice of God saying, Forget it, there are no answers to the questions you're asking, and no place to hide either.

Living in Greece gives rise to this kind of philosophizing, particularly during moonlit nights on small islands like Patmos and even more so in out-of-the-way little farming valleys such as Livádi. There are very few places here to hide, very little buffer between you and reality. Back in the civilized world, most of the more unpleasant aspects of life are cordoned off, sanitized in one way or another. At least before September 11. They always seemed to happen to someone else or on TV, never (in my world, at least) to you. Certainly, you didn't have to check around the toilet before you sat down to make sure there are no black widow spiders nearby, nor worry about losing your foot if you cut it anywhere on an island where not just the fields but the footpaths are sprinkled with manure, animal and human.

Also in the footpaths of this reputed paradise are poisonous snakes (*Vipera berus*), which come out at midday to sun them-selves, barely distinguishable in their grayish-brown inertness from a clump of rocks or the branch of a fig tree. Scorpions are ubiquitous, even showing up in bed with you (as Danielle and I can attest) while you're making love, and in the shallow water of beaches, dragon fish bury themselves in the sand with only their virtually invisible needlelike spines sticking up to impale the unwary foot with extremely painful venom. Same for the sea urchins who lurk, black and bristly, among the rocks.

Accidents, not to mention tragedies, are always just a breath away. A young man you've been having coffee with goes back to work on a dry-docked caïque and, while talking to a buddy, steps into a puddle of water—but the drill he is holding has a loose wire in it and is not grounded. A farmer, the young father of three, buys a new tractor and that same afternoon is crushed beneath it while attempting to drive it on an uneven slope into his field. Funerals are not hidden away in mortuaries and dis-tant cemeteries. The coffin is carried through the village streets at midday, and the women keen, wail, and weep, having no compunction about drowning strangers unmercifully in their sorrow.

So death and afflictions, along with the inbred and mentally challenged, are always sitting at the table, sometimes not such welcome guests but not turned away either or sent to eat in the kitchen. The Greeks have dealt with these things this way since the days of Aeschylus and even before that. It's part of the landscape, along with the beautiful Greek light. And even in the shadows of that light, even at night, there's no place to hide. No matter how nimble you are, one way or the other, reality is going to get you.

So this is the way my thoughts were skittering as I sat on the balcony and looked out at the silent, indifferent landscape, nonetheless magical in the moonlight. Life in the asphalt and concrete comfort of the city of Rethymnon had softened us up a bit, made us think we had some control over events. But now, here we were—

Suddenly, in the house below, the door to the terrace swung open. In the flood of incandescent light that poured forth, I could see Stélios's sturdy silhouette emerge onto the terrace to start the day.

He spotted me immediately.

"Eh, Thomá!" he called out, cheerfully shattering the silence. *"Kalosórisess!"*

Welcome back.

Pentecost

I slipped back into bed and was welcomed by a warm and drowsy Danielle, and we at last rechristened the house by making love. Later that morning after all of us had awoken and were sitting on the terrace having breakfast and enjoying the hot June morning sun, the morbid vapors of my previous night's wanderings again arose when Varvára and Stélios returned from church and presented us with our very own plate of *kóliva*, the sweet and delicious memorial dish of the dead.

Made of boiled wheat kernels mixed with powdered sugar, sesame seeds, slivered almonds, raisins, and pomegranate seeds, *kóliva's* ingredients are redolent of both death and life, of the underworld and the resurrection.

In the Eleusian Mysteries of ancient Greece, a seed of wheat was venerated, hostlike, as a symbol of eternal life, as the "holy grain" of Demeter, the goddess of fertility and of the harvest. The pomegranate, on the other hand, was a symbol of both death and resurrection. The eating of a single seed condemned Persephone, Demeter's daughter, to spend a quarter of the year in the Land of the Dead as the earth above withered and died. But the pomegranate's moist, red, vulvalike interior with its many seeds is also symbolic of life in all its fecundity, and when Persephone returned to earth, she brought the seed with her hidden in her belly.

So today, *kóliva* (page 244) is passed out to Greek Orthodox congregations on occasions such as Pentecost that observe, in one way or another, this cycle of death and rebirth. And in memorial services for the dead, a portion of it is reserved for the deceased so that they can partake of its immortal seeds on their journey to the underworld.

But on Pentecost weekend, the dead are restless, particularly on Saturday, when they know that the following day the season of their resurrection, which they have enjoyed since Holy Thursday, will come to an end, and they will once again be imprisoned in their graves.

Perhaps this is what had given rise to all my restlessness the night before. My father's spirit coming back to warn me against repeating his mistakes, throwing his money away on all those long shots, and the shade of my mother, long since divorced from him, but still shaking her head and saying, "See? Didn't I tell you?"

※

We sat for a while with Varvára and Stélios on their terrace and caught up on the past two years. Things were okay, but Varvára, as always, was uneasy about her heart, which had been weak for years, and the milky-white clouds of glaucoma that were gathering in her sky-blue eyes. She should have had them operated on, but it would have meant going to Athens and leaving Stélios to fend for himself, which worried her. Stélios pooh-

poohed this, but you knew it mattered to him, even though a married daughter, Aryiró, lived just across the other side of the road, not more than two hundred meters away.

Stélios was also beginning to worry about his declining physical abilities, and what would happen to the land and his livestock, their two cows and chickens and turkeys, after he could no longer put in the fifteen hours a day he was now working.

I took the opportunity to ask him how old he was. He grinned, his boyish face spreading almost as wide as the straw hat he had cocked on the back of his head. "Seventy-six, Thomá!"

Varvára smiled. Her hair was silver white. His was still brown, with just a few flecks of gray in it. He was her man.

They had had four children, two daughters and two sons, and as was the custom, the older son and daughter had been free to go off and pursue their own lives, while the two youngest, Aryiró, and her little brother, Stávros, were delegated to remain with their parents. The elder siblings, Theológos and Chrysoúla, went to Athens, where Theológos established a furniture business, and Chrysoúla, whose dowry was the house we were renting, married the owner of a small millinery store.

As soon as Stávros came of age, Stélios had built Aryiró her house across the road, and she had married and gone to live there with her husband, Alékos, the owner of a small café in Upper Livádi. Everything was then set for Stávros to work the farm with Stélios, which he had been doing anyway since he was six, and eventually take it over.

First, however, he had to do his twenty-seven-month tour of duty in the army. Varvára had been very upset about this, but everyone downplayed her anxieties. In those days, relations with Turkey and Yugoslavia were stable, and with no danger of war, what was there to worry about? But you know how mothers are.

Danielle and I had just started living together when we heard the news. Something about a powder magazine exploding. I think it was Alékos and Aryiró who told us, up at the café. Varvára didn't know yet. Stélios didn't know how to tell her.

That evening, we went down to our house as late as we could, just before the fading light made it too dark to negotiate the path, hoping we wouldn't see Varvára. But there she was on her terrace carrying a basket of laundry from a clothesline in back of the house. She smiled and waved to us, as radiant as ever, and disappeared into the house.

About seven the next morning the sudden, rising howl of Varvára's anguish pierced the shutters behind which we were hiding. It was a sound that seemed to come from a place within the human soul too deep and too terrible for any but those who have been forced to go there to ever know about. The hairs stood up on the back of my neck, and our naked bodies stiffened under the sheets. It would be another three hours before we would find the courage to peek out onto the terrace.

Now, as Stélios was talking about the farm and his worries about what might happen to it when he got too old, Varvára looked at us with her clouded blue eyes, and we knew that she was thinking, as we were, about Stávros and all that had been lost with his death.

Between us, on the wooden cover of an olive oil tin used to carry water from the well, sat an untouched dish of *kóliva*.

❋

At eleven o'clock, we headed down to the beach, where many of the people from Livádi would be gathering for coffee and/or lunch at The Beautiful Helen. Varvára and Stélios declined to join us. In the seven years I had lived there, I don't remember them ever coming down to Theológos's. Their direction had always been up, in spite of Varvára's bad heart, on foot, to the tiny square outside the church, where their grandchildren played and worked in Aryiró's husband's café. But they promised that when I started cooking, they would definitely come for a meal. *"Éhomeh kayró,"* they said. "We have time."

Ever on Sunday

Overnight, something miraculous had happened to The Beautiful Helen. It had been transformed from a dingy mortuary housing the detritus of the previous summer into a lively near-replica of the Helen of my memory and my dreams.

Part of the metamorphosis came from the sunlight now pouring into it across the glittering waters of the bay and shimmering on the walls and ceiling, brightening even the hospital-green paint on the walls. The rest of the change came from the job of resurrection that Theológos and Démetra and the boys had done on everything else.

All the stacked tables and chairs had been outfitted with flowered plastic coverings and set in the outside and inside dining areas. And both of the glass-fronted refrigerators had been filled with a colorful array of beer, wine, and soft drinks, bowls and plates of appetizers such as an Eggplant Dip (*melitzáno-saláta*) (page 208), and the Yogurt, Cucumber, and Garlic Dip (*tzatzíki*) (page 206). There was also a selection of meat and fish revitalized from the ice-cream freezer, just in case there happened to be a high roller among the customers, which there nearly always was, someone who would see those items and just have to show his fellow islanders how flush he was—or, anyway, felt.

Back by the kitchen, Theológos, a white dish towel slung over the shoulder of his near-immaculate white shirt, was barking out orders to Lámbros and Sávas as they scurried back and forth between the kitchen and the customers. Only Démetra had time to grace us with a genuinely interested smile and a cheery good morning, her gold-capped tooth flashing amid the steam from the crusted-black casseroles that she was tending to on top of the stove, their contents wreathing us with the tantalizing aromas of the dill-and-lemon-flavored meatballs of a dish called *youvarlákia avgolémono* (Meatballs in Egg-Lemon Sauce, page 220) and cinnamon-spiced *moschári stifádo* (Eléni's Veal Stew, page 240).

In a corner, the lugubrious voice of a Greek male pop singer moaning love lyrics came from an ancient jukebox, its volume control up to the highest possible level, as, at the tables, a crowd of Patmians, energized by the noise, happily shouted to one another across both the tables and the dining area, using up all that was left of the decibel spectrum.

It was the end of a strict religious observance that had begun ninety days before in the Lenten bleakness of March and was at last being lifted in today's bright summer sunshine. On Patmos, permeated as it is by its own sanctity as the site of God's revelations to St. John and by the rhythms and hours of the monastery, these observances are taken with the utmost seriousness by a near-total majority of the populace.

But when they finish with it, they finish with it. And go back out into the world with as renewed a vigor as the apostles had shown on the first Pentecost when the fire of the Holy Spirit had descended upon them, giving them the power to speak in tongues. They were so enthused by their mission that St. Peter was forced to defend them against charges of drunkenness. "These men are not drunk," he indignantly protested. "It is only nine in the morning!"

Well, here at The Beautiful Helen, it was a little after eleven and at least some of the assembled Patmians were certainly well on their way, tabletops already filling with an increasingly impressive display of empty beer bottles, testament to both their financial largesse (beer being the most expensive drink you could buy) as well as their staying powers and general joy in the occasion.

Danielle and I knew everyone present and, after effusive greetings and inquiries about the health of the children and Danielle's parents, who had visited five summers before, we were invited to sit at a dozen tables, but at the same time, not pressed to do so. If either of us had been alone, we would have had no choice—in such a tight-knit community, sitting (and eating and drinking) by yourself is nearly out of the question, but if you are a foreign friend, it is anathema. The famous hospitality of the Greeks is not overblown tourist hype. It's what Lawrence Durrell calls an "iron law" and is deeply rooted in the Greek national character. The Greek word *xénos* means not only stranger or foreigner (as in xenophobia) but also, with equal emphasis, guest, as in the Greek for hotel, *xenodoheéon.*

"Yeah," says an Italian-American friend of mine, whose husband is Greek, "if you're a guest in their house, they'll give you the shirt off their back. But do business with them, it's *your* shirt you've got to worry about!"

"Élla, Thomá! Daniélla!" our old friends shouted from their tables—graying, curly-haired Michális, the man who had put a new roof on our farmhouse; his cousin, Theológos, who'd put in the windows; club-footed Poditós, who sold us our fish straight from his fishing boat; and toothless Yerásimos, who had farmed our land and made wine from our tiny vineyard, plus half a dozen other *Livadióti*—*"Na sas keráso!"* they said. "Come! I'll treat you!"

I was mightily tempted, not only because I wanted to shake off the dour cobwebs of the night before but because I was beginning to emerge from the cocoon of a winter of teaching in Rethymnon and wanted to fling myself headlong into being back on Patmos in the summer.

Danielle, ever alert to these impulses, politely declined each invitation to sit and gradually steered us to a table on the edge of the terrace, where we could eat and drink at our own pace. While she had never begrudged the gregarious side of my nature, she nevertheless wanted to make sure we all got a good meal in before I went off on my rounds of renewing acquaintances.

The truth was that although she loved the tavérna and its proximity to the beach and sea, she had never much liked going there except in the early mornings and off season, when there would be almost no one around but Theológos, Eléni, and the boys, and maybe a few grizzled fishermen. As soon as the season started, and it became crowded, she would stay only long enough to get Sara and herself something to eat. And then, while I presided over an ever-burgeoning congregation of friends and new acquaintances from Holland, Germany, Austria, Israel, and the States, she would go off to a corner of the beach and sit for hours, reading or staring out at the sea, cigarette dangling from her lips, as Sara waddled along the water's edge.

Paradoxically, this was one of the reasons why I had fallen in love with her—because she could do with ease what I found so difficult: to say no to all the distractions and temptations, the tumult and confusions of the world, and slip into the seclusion of herself and her art, where she could think and work at her own rhythm in utter peace and quiet. In this way, she embodied what had originally attracted me about Patmos—that it was an island for solitaries and solitudes, for caves and inward revelations. But there was Patmos's other side, too, its secular, worldly life—that of its Cretan forebears and the *mágus* Yénoupas— which was continually and increasingly, particularly with the advent of the new pier, putting itself in the forefront, pulsating with attractions. And I, in contrast to Danielle, was (and am) always terrified that I'm going to miss something—especially, I must confess, the kinds of things I suspect may be bad for me.

So I let her lead us out of the welcoming crowd at The Beautiful Helen and to a table at the edge of the dining area. But within minutes, I was up and off to the kitchen to bring us something to drink and to see more of what was cooking on the back burners of the huge black stove that Démetra was attending.

We had the *youvarlákia avgolémono* (Meatballs in Egg-Lemon Sauce) and a *horiátiki saláta*, the famous Greek "peasant salad" with feta cheese, particularly delicious when the ingredients come from the ground right outside the tavérna; tomatoes stuffed with herbs and rice; and the ubiquitous, indispensable *patátess tiganitéss* (French-fried potatoes). After we had finished, Danielle went off with the children to wander along the beach, leaving me unencumbered to satisfy all of my baser table-hopping instincts and, today at least, get the reintroductions out of the way.

By this time, of course, I was nearly frothing at the mouth to tell the people of valley about the plans I had for the tavérna. So, I was rendered almost speechless to discover that none of them had been told why we were there. Apparently, Theológos had decided to keep counsel only with himself. Knowing what I knew about the Greeks' distrust of one another, I probably should have kept my mouth shut, too. But, American that I am, if I have some good news, I have to tell the world. It was a habit I had persisted in even after I'd observed how uncomfortable even my closest Greek friends became whenever I made such announcements.

This closemouthedness has a lot to do with their belief in the power of the evil eye, *toh kakó máhti*, which arises from envy. Although there are people who can deliberately give it to you—especially women, and especially those with blue eyes—

its malevolent effects can be set in motion even by someone innocently wanting or valuing something that you have, such as a new car or a better job. The consequences of being struck by the evil eye can be dire, ranging from a string of minor mishaps to major misfortunes, from a persistent, unidentifiable feeling of depression to a serious and possibly fatal illness.

Therefore, you must try to hide your good fortune and certainly never crow over it. Even better is to take extra precautions by openly and loudly belittling anything you have that you think might cause envy. This is why many of the women in Rethymnon, to whom we proudly displayed our newly born son, had demonstrated their true feelings for him (and their horror at our open display of hubris) by contemptuously spitting at our feet. I was within a millisecond of physically assaulting the first little old lady who did this before I understood what was happening.

This is also why it is almost impossible to get anyone in the country to congratulate you about anything. An announcement such as "I sold my novel!" is greeted by an embarrassed silence as your Greek friends look at the ground, searching for a way to change the subject.

While my higher faculties tell me that I don't really believe in such things, there's another part of me that wants to pay it due respect anyway, much as I used to pray for my soul before I went to sleep, and even now throw salt over my shoulder—just in case. As a famous physicist once said, when someone accused him of being superstitious because he had a horseshoe hanging on his wall, "Well, they say it works even if you don't believe."

Nevertheless, on this particular afternoon, I had no intention of cowering. After all, it was Pentecost Sunday, wasn't it? And the Holy Spirit was upon us—or in my case, *kéfi* seemed to be, which is almost the same thing and fully capable of protecting you against the evil eye. Or at least, that's what I was determined to believe.

In contrast to the *kakó máhti*, which is man-made, *kéfi* is a gift from the gods and can best be described as possession by the spirit of happiness, that of Dionysos, I suspect, the god of wine, orgies, and whatever else turns you on. As I have written in my *Essential Greek Handbook*, it cannot be deliberately summoned, say by drinking and dancing, but suddenly descends upon you without warning, infuses you with joy, and then, when it has run its course, disappears, perhaps not to return again for another year or even a lifetime. In other words, it is very much like what the Christians call grace.

Greeks can instantly recognize if someone has *kéfi* and treat the person so blessed with a great deal of deference, allowing that individual to do almost anything he or she wishes—such as expressing high spirits by tossing a chair through the window—without censure.

Did I have *kéfi* that afternoon? I may have thought so, but my Greek friends didn't. Instead of indulging my whims and telling me how delighted they were that I was going to be running The Beautiful Helen that summer and buying me drinks on it, they all took me aside during the course of the afternoon, privately, one by one, and to a man told me to watch myself. *"Kléftis eénay!"* they said of Theológos, *O Ladós*. "He's a thief."

But I had already been down this road with Melyá and come to the conclusion that since the Greeks consider all Greeks thieves and liars, you can't even trust the advice of the ones who are warning you about the others. What are *their* motives? Envy? Or, in this instance, was there also a bit of anti-Americanism in there somewhere? You could go nuts trying to figure it out. So I was just going to break this vicious cycle by plunging in and trusting someone, i.e., Theológos, who anyway already had my hundred and fifty thousand drachmas deep in his pocket.

But I didn't tell my Greek friends this. Instead, I thanked them for their advice and promised to watch myself.

By this time, it was midafternoon, and Danielle and the kids had tired of the beach. They said they wanted to go back to the house for a nap. But a renewed spirit, a second wind, had descended upon me, equal parts Greek beer and American conviviality, and I decided it would be in the best interests of my future business affairs to stay in the tavérna and make my potential customers feel at home. By now these included not only my Patmian friends but various tourists who had wandered by and decided to join in the festivities.

So while my family went off to rest, I remained throughout the rest of the afternoon, speaking in foreign tongues, tempting my audience with visions of the meals I would create, and picturing the multitude of customers who would flock to the tavérna day and night once they discovered that they could at last get not only a good meal on the island, but an exotic one as well: French, Italian, Chinese, Indian, Tex-Mex, you name it! I would even take special orders!

As the drinking of beer slipped into retsina and ouzo, my recollections of what went on during the rest of the afternoon become a bit hazy. At one point, I do remember Evripídes driving up in his new taxi (by this time, the old *aeropláno* had been put out to pasture, lovingly preserved in a cinder-block, plastic-roofed enclosure especially built for her), and as he slowed down on the road in front of the tavérna, I glimpsed what I thought was Melyá in the shadows of the backseat, her blond hair glowing faintly in the ambient light. She was wearing sunglasses, so I don't know if she saw me, but Evripídes was only able to get out a quick *"Yásoo, Thomá!"* before he was impelled to drive on.

When Danielle and the children returned about six, I was still on fire and had by this time dragged a box of my kitchen supplies out into the main room. When they walked in, I was entertaining Theológos, Démetra, Lámbros, Sávas, and the few customers who were still there with an extravagant demonstration of how a Cuisinart food processor—which I had miraculously found on a dusty back shelf of a store in Rethymnon—could not only chop onions and parsley but grind raw meat as well.

When blond-haired Lámbros commented on what a beautiful American *prágma,* thing, it was, Danielle smiled.

"Galikó eénay," she said. "It's French." Then she looked at me and smiled again. "Like the Statue of Liberty."

For dinner, we had crisp and succulent Greek *keftédes* (Greek Meatballs, page 218), made with the beef, onion, and parsley I had put through the processor and then seasoned myself with a touch of mint, cinnamon, nutmeg, and cayenne.

By nine-thirty, we were back in our house on the hill, snug in our beds like Varvára, Stélios, and their cows, donkeys, and chickens, just after the light of dusk had finally faded from the sky.

And it was as if we had never been away.

The House on the Hill—II

For the first three months of my first summer in Livádi, from May until the beginning of August, I lived as I had promised myself I would, holed up in that house on the hill like one of those hermit-monks who cling to the holy slopes of Mount Athos and Metéora, hardly leaving except to go down to The Beautiful Helen for lunch and to make weekly shopping expeditions into Skála.

When I was in Skála, I kept away from foreign contact, taking the back streets to the grocery stores and bakery so I wouldn't have to chance striking up a conversation. To fortify my spiritual side, I bought books about the Apocalypse and pictures of the icons in the Monastery of St. John. I even went so far as to bring home several of the little oil lamps the Greeks use to illuminate the icons, and occasionally fired up incense to make my room smell like a church. In the meantime, I lost nearly twenty-five pounds eating at the tavérna and out of Stélios's garden, the fat from the multiple martini pre-show dinners and hot pastrami sandwiches I had had in Manhattan melting from my body.

The pages of my novel, a re-setting of Dostoevsky's *Crime and Punishment* in Vietnam, began piling up on the window ledge in front of my desk where I could see them, fruits of my virtuous labors, as I gazed out at the violet and azure sea.

In those days, I had The Beautiful Helen virtually all to myself. At noon I would come down to the beach and sit like a king under its thick tamarisk tree, waited on hand and foot by tiny Lámbros and Sávas while their sister and mother busied themselves in the kitchen.

Eléni, I learned, was from the north of Greece. Like the other Helen in the Trojan War, she had been spirited by her suitor away from her family and brought to make a home in this "foreign" land. The dishes she cooked were flavored with the exotic Levantine spices favored by cooks from her region— cinnamon, nutmeg, cumin, and allspice—and often cooked in sweet red wine. Every day there would be something tasty and substantial to eat: *papoutzákia* or *imám bayaldí,* for example, meat-and-eggplant dishes scented with spices and swimming in an oil-rich tomato sauce, or *octopódi stifádo,* octopus stew, and *briam,* an oven-baked vegetable casserole heady with oregano and garlic.

Theodóra, the daughter, was just beginning to blossom into adolescence, hiding from sight in the kitchen, standing off in corners and rarely looking up from her work, yet taking in everything behind her lowered lashes. In contrast, Sávas, six, and Lámbros, five, were as bright-eyed and eager as squirrels, ready to pounce on every scrap of information they could get from me, this exotic *kírios*, gentleman, from America who had chosen their valley in which to spend his summer.

While waiting for lunch, I would play the finger games and magic tricks that my father and uncle had taught me as a child, and let them listen to my Walkman, educating them in Western music by playing tapes of the Beatles and Bob Dylan.

During the weekdays, Theológos was usually absent, off in his caïque on Important Business Matters, sometimes only to Skála, but on occasion as far as Samos, a four-hour trip to the north, or Piraeus and Athens, gathering provisions.

In those days, the summer season did not begin until July 1, when the families who owned vacation houses in the valley and along the beach would start arriving from their winter homes in Skála and Hóra, and as far away as Athens and Australia. But this influx hardly made a ripple on the tranquillity of the days or on my monklike existence. They would look at me with curiosity, and after a while, even began to nod when I came down to the beach, but otherwise they barely noticed me. While most were clearly not wealthy, they had a certain patrician attitude toward Livádi. This was their valley and their beach and had been for generation upon generation, probably back until sometime in the twelfth century, when their families, many descended from the upper echelons of medieval Byzantine society, had first chosen Livádi as their summer retreat. Thus Theológos, who had been born on the hardscrabble, windswept north of the island, the son of dirt-poor farmers, was regarded as something of an interloper, albeit, because of his tavérna, a useful one. As for me, I was just a passing phenomenon, like so many other foreign visitors before me, an interesting distraction perhaps—as long as I didn't make waves, like the marauding Venetians or the Italians and Nazis—but with the staying power, like them, of a fly in summer.

Only on Sundays, when the working islanders and local *Livadióti* would have time to visit, was there anything even faintly resembling a crowd at the beach, and only then would Theológos be sure to be there for lunch, ready to set up extra tables on the tree-shaded beach, dish towel draped over his shoulder, face florid from the heat. When customers came on the other days or evenings that he was present, he let Eléni and the children do the work, and played the affable host, making his guests feel at home, sitting to talk with them at their tables, and sharing a coffee or an ouzo, the pasha in residence.

After lunch, I would go back to my cave and nap and then get up and work again. The afternoons were languorous and hot, with never a cloud darkening the sky, the silence broken only by the sounds of livestock and by an occasional shout from one distant house to another about some domestic matter: "Varvára?! Do you have any sugar?!" Dinner was at about seven and when the lights of all the houses went out at about nine, the ensuing darkness was so complete, the stars shining in such intense multitudes, that you felt you had traveled to another part of the universe.

But throughout the tranquillity of all these works and days, there was always in the back of my mind the memory of that young Frenchwoman I had seen sitting in a café in Skála with a glass of ouzo beside her, her perfectly formed breasts free in a thin cotton T-shirt as she leaned slightly forward and stared with almond-shaped eyes at something only they could see— and I was dying to know about.

Cuisine Arts

The morning after Pentecost Sunday, I went down to The Beautiful Helen to sort through the rest of my belongings and show off some of the other wonders I had brought from

Rethymnon. As I was sitting on the floor with Sávas and Lámbros, surrounded by opened boxes like kids at Christmas, Theológos returned from a shopping trip to Skála and immediately picked up where he had left off months before in Rethymnon.

"You brought those?!" he cried, pointing at a four-pound sack of kidney beans, which was peeking out of a box.

"I want to give them a try," I said. "I'm sure—"

"*Keéta*, look!" he shouted to several fishermen who were having coffee in the dining area.

They came into the kitchen, as did Démetra and her younger brother, sunny, curly-locked Mémis, newly returned from the army, who was helping clean the kitchen.

Theológos lifted the sack of kidney beans. "In America, people eat these!"

"Not just America," I said. "Also Mexico and—"

"Thomá," Démetra said, as if speaking to a child, "these are for animals."

"I know that," I replied, patiently, "but not in America and Mexico. We make wonderful dishes from them. *Poleé nóstimo!* Delicious! For instance, we fry them."

"Fry them?!" exclaimed Poditós, one of the fishermen.

"Thomá—they're very hard," Sávas said, helpfully.

"First," I replied, thin-lipped, "we boil them."

"Good!" said Démetra's brother, Mémis, with unmerited enthusiasm.

"Then we make a puree," I continued, "and mash them down and fry them."

"Ah!" said Poditós. "And—?"

"Then," I hesitated, suddenly aware of what I was getting into, "we—uh—fry them some more."

"Why?"

I looked at him and then at Theológos, who just stood there grinning.

"Never mind," I muttered. "Anyway, that's not what I'm going to do."

"Good!" cried Mémis again as Démetra, barely able to suppress a grin, dug her elbow in his side.

The morning sun, bouncing off the sea, was making aqueous ripples on the ceiling as I looked up at the *Livadióti*, my Greek chorus. I was kneeling next to Theológos's immense walk-in refrigerator, where the boxes had been stored since our arrival Saturday night.

This refrigerator—which took up about one quarter of the entire kitchen—was typical of some of the other improvements Theológos had made in his tavérna. He had bought it dirt cheap off a friend who had gotten it from a man in Athens who was refurbishing the interior of a freighter, had somehow transported it to Patmos and Livádi, dismantled the front wall of the tavérna to get it inside, and then barely had a chance to try it out when it broke down forever. It was now used as a storage room, its shadowy galvanized interior stuffed with boxes and crates, old clothes hanging on meat hooks, and a jumble of battered tools and paint-spattered footwear on the floor.

As I was being interrogated about the kidney beans, I began to feel a sudden kinship with that refrigerator. If I wasn't careful, I too would suffer a similar fate and be broken down into a repository for the old and familiar.

I rummaged through another box, an emergency package airmailed by friends in New York. It was filled with goodies almost unobtainable in Greece: soy sauce, powdered ginger, turmeric, green, black, and white peppercorns, cardamom pods, cardamom powder, coriander, garam masala, and Coomaraswamy's curry powder. I found what I wanted and held up a bottle of Gebhardt's Chili Powder.

"Special spices from Texas!" I said. "With these, I will make a wonderful casserole of the beans stewed with ground beef, tomatoes, onions, tomato paste, wine, et cetera. *Poleé nóstimo!* You will see."

"Yes," agreed Theológos. "We will see!"

Lámbros, Theológos's younger son, gave me an encouraging smile. "Probably it will be good," he ventured.

Sávas touched the food processor. "And this is wonderful!" he said, encouragingly.

Mémis shrugged. *"O tee théli O Theh-ós!"* he proclaimed. "Whatever God wants!"

I had been gathering items for the tavérna virtually since that day in January when Theológos had called to offer it to me, and coming across the food processor in Rethymnon had certainly seemed like a godsend. It was an original, professional model Cuisinart Culinaire and had been gathering dust in the nether regions of a kitchenware store for years. The little old woman who was handling things while her husband was away in Athens immediately knew, when she saw the surprised and unguarded eagerness of my expression, that she had at last found a sucker.

"It likes you?" she asked in the Greek way, in which the verb "to like" is reflexive. *"S'arési?"*

I hesitated, and she immediately lowered the price by a couple of thousand drachmas, no doubt just to be able to tell her husband that she'd finally gotten rid of his white elephant.

In turn, I was realizing that the amount written on the box must have been calculated several years before when the drachma had been worth about four times more than its present value. Therefore, I was not so much hesitating as catching my breath, figuring that if I kept my mouth shut and abandoned the Cherry Tree Principle of Conduct, I could get it for next to nothing. So when she took that two thousand off, I immediately agreed, thanking her profusely. I think I even mentioned how fortunate our poor little children would be to have such a wonderful machine to puree their food.

The little old lady smiled happily. So did I. Together we had achieved a rare pinnacle of perfection in Greek business dealings: that special moment when both the buyer and the seller are convinced they have thoroughly bamboozled the other.

Yes, the finding of the processor had been most providential. Not only had it proven to me that I could put something over on a Greek (and believe me, those little old ladies in black are a lot tougher than they look), but it seemed a clear sign that God was on my side—something that we Americans always like to be reassured of, particularly in our dealings with foreigners.

In addition to the spices and food processor, I had also brought a number of other "modern" devices with me, including a garlic press, vegetable peeler, pepper grinder, measuring cups and spoons, two food timers, and a device for cutting perfect French fries by pushing whole potatoes lengthwise through a razor-sharp grid. So I felt fairly well equipped for what I could now see was going to have to be a prolonged assault on the Old Way of Doing Things.

While the Greeks are like kids in a toy shop when it comes to newfangled items such as cell phones, they put up massive Mycenean walls if you try to criticize or fiddle with their culinary ways. Not only have these recipes and methods been reverently handed down as home cooking from generation to generation but they supposedly go back to the time of Socrates and before, when they, the Greeks, claim to have invented haute cuisine.

Amazingly, there is considerable evidence to support this contention. Even as early as *The Iliad* and *The Odyssey* (c. 750 B.C.), Homer was devoting an inordinate number of lines to describing various feasts or other eating occasions, including a section on Achilles making *souvlákia* (shish kebab to you and the Turks) out of skewered goat and pig's back and grilling them over embers on the beach at Troy. In addition, one of the world's earliest known cookbooks was written by a Sicilian Greek named Mithaecus, a chef so famous that Plato mentions him in his *Gorgias,* calling his dishes "exquisite." Plato also pointed out that food and drink were among the three all-consuming passions of ancient Athens, the third not being philosophy, as you may have thought, but sex.

Classical Athens also saw the development of what were most certainly the precursors of today's eateries—some twenty-three hundred years before the French claim they came up with the restaurant in post-Bastille Paris—where Athenians of the poorer classes, who didn't have enough room at home for a dinner party, could sit and air their opinions over a carafe or two.

Originally, these establishments were shops selling wine and vinegar in bulk. Since you had to have a leisurely, thoughtful taste of the wine before buying, tables and chairs were no doubt provided, and later a few *mezés,* appetizers, to improve the tasting, and finally, home-cooked meals. Interestingly, in those days, too, there were warnings about the untrustworthiness of the owners, with the comic playwright Aristophanes having some barbed remarks to make about the way they tried to cheat you in their measures, giving less than you paid for.

But somewhere in the course of history, most likely during the four-hundred-year Ottoman domination, when many Greeks became the chefs of their overlords and acquired a knowledge of Turkish dishes that they now consider Greek— such as *imám balyidí* (which means "the imam [a Muslim priest] fainted" in Turkish, probably because of the cost of the expensive olive oil employed)—the majority of the Greeks threw culinary refinement out the window and opted for food as mere fuel, without the frills, particularly the expensive ones. Nowadays, with the exception of the higher-class establishments in Athens and Thessaloníki (where there are superb restaurants) and some resort areas, most other places are extremely cavalier about the quality of their dishes, more often than not serving them lukewarm, somewhat old, limp, and oily.

So when Mémis exclaimed, "Whatever God wants!"—that national sigh of resignation—my back immediately went up. Maybe in your world, I thought, but not in mine!

Countdown

"Now, Thomá," said Theológos, sitting down beside me with a pencil and paper in hand. "Tell me what *you* want."

We were at a corner table inside the tavérna. It was later that same Monday morning, and the sun was now bouncing off the sand and the dusty concrete of the terrace, suffusing the interior with a warm, beige light. Outside, a few tourists were quietly having late breakfasts as Démetra and the boys saw to their needs.

"I will go to Athens tomorrow," Theológos continued, "and come back on Friday. What do you want me to bring? Beer, soft drinks, sparkling water, wine, beef? I can get you very good frozen meats, cheap—chicken, too—tomato paste, potatoes, onions? What do you need? And how much?"

"Well," I said, trying to muster up a semblance of knowing what I was talking about, "You know—the usual!"

He gave me a brief look, then smiled.

"Thomá," he said gently, "*you* also must know. You must learn to count what's on hand—the drinks, the meats, the vegetables, the eggs, cheese, salt, pepper, spices, napkins—"

"Theológo, I can't do all that and—"

"You run a tavérna, you have to."

"We're in this fifty-fifty—"

"That doesn't matter. *You* still have to know. For your own good." He paused, fixed me in his sights, and said, "Suppose I try to cheat you?"

I stared at him, speechless, barely able to take this in and definitely not knowing how to respond. I hate confrontations and would never in a million years have brought it up. But suddenly, there it was.

I took a deep breath.

"Look, Theológo," I said. "A lot of people have been warning me about you, telling me not to trust you, that you'll steal from me—"

He smiled. "*O Ladós?*"

I stared at him. For some absurd reason, I'd thought he would assume I didn't know about his nickname.

"Yes," I said.

"And?"

"I don't believe them."

He didn't bat an eye, just continued to look at me, searching my face for clues of what I was really thinking.

"We've been friends for years," I continued. "You wouldn't do that to me. I know that. So the hell with them. They're jealous!"

A faint smile came into his dark brown eyes, flecked with gold from the reflected sunlight.

"I'll do the cooking," I said, "and you do the counting and buying. I trust you. And you're better at it anyway. Okay?"

"You're sure?" he said, again searching my face.

I stuck out my hand. "Sure."

He hesitated, then put his hand in mine, and we shook on it. His hand was rough and callused from the work he had been doing since childhood, the ropes and picks and saws and hammers he had handled, and now it felt nearly inhuman, a paw chiseled from rock.

We ordered another cup of coffee to seal our new arrangement, and then I gave him a list of items I wanted for my specialties (making no mention, of course, of the chili) and left it for him to decide what else was needed.

He made some quick calculations.

"Okay," he said. "Now, you give me, let's say, ten thousand drachmas for the trip, and I'll—"

"Ten thousand drachmas!" I screamed. Although only a little more than two hundred dollars, ten thousand drachmas was, in those days and on that island, still a considerable sum.

"It includes half the cost of my boat ticket," explained Theológos, "a hotel room, cheap, and—"

"But I already gave you a hundred and fifty thousand!"

He looked at me, a pained expression on his face. "Thomá," he patiently explained, "that was just the rent."

I stared at him. Just the rent . . .

At that moment, a Jeep and then two motorcycles skidded to a halt outside the tavérna, raising a cloud of sand and dust over the breakfasting customers. Out of the cloud emerged a pride of Nordic males in their thirties and forties, all bleary-eyed and unshaven, their pale, slightly paunchy bodies dressed in various versions of the latest in Scandinavian swimwear.

Accompanying them was a fresh-faced blonde in her early twenties, very beautiful. A model or an actress no doubt, she was tastefully attired in a man's white shirt and a woman's very brief bikini bottom.

In sharp contrast was the apparition who stumbled out of the Jeep behind her. She was a stunning creature in her late thirties, her Shirley Temple curls, under a white Carmen Miranda turban, dyed a shimmering orangish, copper red. She was wearing full makeup, huge, white-rimmed Holly Golightly sunglasses, platform rope-soled sandals, and a Donald Duck beach towel.

"Oh, oh," said Theológos. We glanced at each other.

The men burst through the door of the tavérna, looked around, spotted me, and one of them shouted, "Thomá! Melyá told us you were here!"

Drink, Food, Sex

They were Norwegians. Two of the men—square-jawed Magnus, a news and fashion photographer, and angular, towheaded Jens, whose father built pleasure boats—I had known since Mykonos, ten years before. The other two, the bikers, were in the European film business, in some obscure technical capacity that still made them enough money to spend two months a year on Patmos.

The redhead, Lili, another old friend, also had something to do with the movie business, but you could never pin her down as to exactly what. She always seemed to have lots of free time and, like Garbo, liked to maintain a certain distance. When we had first met, and I had asked my standard question, "What do you do in real life?" she had turned her sunglasses on me and smiled.

"As little as possible," she said in that deep Greta-like voice of hers.

The young blonde, Anna, seemed to be simply the latest in an ever-changing line of women Magnus regularly brought with him on his summer visits. Inevitably, they were models. Anna, however, was in graduate school, a budding lawyer. Perhaps she would turn out, at last, to be the One.

Lili smiled at me. "Where's Danielle?"

"In the house setting up her paints and things," I said. "With our children."

"Oh, that's right," said Lili. "You have two now! Are you *never* going to be free?"

We had moved outside to the terrace and were having our first drinks of the day. At least, Magnus, Jens, and I were, doing what we had done every summer, consecrating the rebirth of the season with what was certain to be a long afternoon of beers and retsina and talk.

It was part of a series of such rituals that those of us who lived on Greek islands had to go through every time an old friend visited. When you are a resident winter and summer, you are, ipso facto, a host, and therefore expected to be not only delighted by your friends' arrivals but ready to celebrate them too—each one as though it were your first of the year. Needless to say, by August, this starts to wreak serious havoc on the liver, particularly if you have friends arriving weekly. At forty-two, I didn't at all feel over the hill, but on this particular morning, with the festivities of Pentecost Sunday just behind me, I was beginning to suspect that my body's ability to recover was not what it once was. Still, you can't say no, not to old friends like these.

I asked about Melyá.

"What's going on between you two?" said Magnus.

"What did she say?"

"Nothing. Except, 'I don't want to talk about it.'"

I explained, in detail, what had happened. "So she thinks Theológos and I are in a conspiracy to keep her out."

"Aren't you?"

"*No!*"

Europeans are a lot like the Greeks. They don't believe people tell the truth. Nobody believes this except we Americans—and I'm not so sure about us anymore, not these days.

"Don't worry," said Magnus. "She'll come around. She always does."

Maybe not this time, I thought.

"So what kind of food are you going to serve?" asked Anna.

I smiled at her, grateful for the change of subject. Even though I knew I was in the right about Melyá, I still felt that I had somehow betrayed her and should have let Theológos rent the tavérna to someone else, purely on principle. Even though nobody much believes in principles anymore either.

I happily launched into a detailed description of the menu, and then said, "The opening is next Monday. Bring lots of people!"

There was a silence.

"We can't," said Magnus.

"Why?!"

"We just flew down for a week," said Jens.

"We got together for a drink in Oslo a week ago Friday—" said Gunnar.

"First time we'd all seen each other since last summer," Magnus added.

Helmut grinned. "We got a little drunk. You know . . ."

"And the next thing I knew," said Anna, "I was on a plane to Greece! I couldn't believe it!" She took Magnus's arm and smiled at him. He patted her hand.

"We have to leave Sunday," he said. "We all have work next day."

"Not me," intoned Lili. "*I* shall be at your opening!"

"Thank you," I said.

"And we'll be back later in the summer," promised Magnus.

"Thomá?" Theológos was at the tavérna door. He motioned for me to come inside.

I excused myself.

Theológos took me to the outside storage area behind the kitchen, where there were piles of crates and empty bottles. "I have counted everything. People drank up a lot on Sunday. We don't have as much as I thought. I'll need about fifteen thousand from you for the trip. Okay?"

"Theológo—"

"Here are the figures." He held out a slip of the gray scrap paper that the Greeks used for writing bills in places without cash registers. It was covered on both sides with numbers and with scrawls in written Greek, something so unlike the printed kind that, to me, it might as well have been Arabic.

I gazed at this mess, incomprehensible except for a final, cir-
cled figure of *30,000 drs.,* and said nothing.

"You don't have to give it all to me now," Theológos continued. "You have ten thousand?"

"I have five," I said.

He looked hurt.

"Okay," I said. "Eight."

He brightened.

"The rest I will give you from the first week's profits," I said.
"All right?"

"No problem, Thomá!" Theológos answered expansively, in
English. He grinned and clapped me on the shoulder. "Don't
worry! I trust you!"

I went back to our table and was just sitting down when
there came another shout from inside the tavérna.

"Thomá!"

Mémis, Démetra's younger brother, burst out of the doorway and headed for our table. He was naked to the waist, his
hairless, bronzed, and slightly plump torso gleaming with a
thin sheen of sweat, barefoot, a pair of baggy khakis hanging on
his hips, curly blond hair bouncing on his head. He was holding the shiny stainless steel French-fry cutter in one hand and a
large peeled potato in the other. "Look!"

Without bothering to even acknowledge the presence of
anyone else at the table, he cleared a space in front of me and
positioned the cutter. Then he placed the potato in the slot,
grabbed the base with his left hand, and, with his right,
slammed down the cutter's handle. A barrage of perfectly cut
French fries shot out across the plastic tablecloth.

Mémis beamed. "Good, yes?!" he cried in English.

"Beautiful!" I said.

He smiled at everyone else. "Beau-ti-ful!"

Then he looked down at the potatoes scattered among the
beers and coffees.

"Oh, *pardón!*"

He quickly swept the cut potatoes into his hands and, putting the cutter under his arm, said *"Pardón!"* again and backed toward the doorway, stopping to smile at us one last time before disappearing into the shadows of the interior.

There was a moment of silence, and then Lili swung her sunglasses around to me, a slight smile on her bright red lips. "Who he?"

"Lili—" said Magnus.

"Just a simple question," she said.

"He's Démetra's brother," I replied. "He's been in the army."

"Ah!"

"Tom?" It was Anna.

"Yes?"

"Why don't you open this Saturday?"

I looked at her.

"Yes," said Magnus. "Why not? It's only two days' difference."

"Ask Theológos," said Gunnar.

"Tell him we'll bring friends," said Lili. "Twenty people."

I hesitated.

"Please," said Anna. "Maybe this is my only chance. Maybe I can't come back later in the summer."

"Ask him," said Gunnar again.

As if summoned by fate, Theológos appeared in the doorway, scratching his stomach, his undershirt stained with sweat. I called him over, gesturing toward the Norwegians.

"Theológo," I said, "they are leaving Sunday night. They will miss my opening."

"Can't he start on Saturday?" asked Lili.

Theológos looked at her.

"Please," said beautiful Anna.

"We'll bring lots of people," added Magnus.

"A big party!" said Jens.

Theológos smiled. Then he looked at me. And then back at the others, savoring the suspense. He grinned. "You are my friends. For my friends—what you want!"

"Bravo, Theológo!" we shouted, raising our glasses.

Démetra, Mémis, Lámbros, and Sávas, looking on from the doorway, glowed.

And at this moment, Danielle and the children turned the corner of the path from our house, and Sara rushed into my arms, with a happy, gurgling Matt trundling after.

It was already promising to be quite a summer.

First Lessons

That Saturday morning, I unpacked the rest of my things and began making a space for myself in the kitchen.

It was, of course, infinitely smaller than the one I had remembered when I was indulging in my fantasies back in Rethymnon. Barely large enough to accommodate tiny Démetra and myself, much less Mémis and the boys, every available space in it seemed to be utilized twice over. The walls were lined with shelves, cupboards, and counters and crammed with pots, pans, casseroles, plates, glasses, flour, pastas, herbs, matches, old lottery tickets, nails, string, and, among other useless items, a broken telephone. In the center stood a large working table, and another, smaller table was in a nook leading to the glass-fronted display units. Along the back wall crouched a huge, blackened electric stove and oven with four hot plates on top. Next to it was a gas-operated three-burner range.

To the left of the stove, also along the back wall, were two stained, stainless steel sinks and a draining board, and leading off that to the rear, a long, narrow space that Theológos had recently added on in one of his attempts at improvement. It was a bedroom, dressing and storage room, with two narrow cots that were used both for quick naps and for the boys to sleep in at night. A narrow passageway running behind the walk-in refrigerator linked it to the tavérna's single toilet, also accessible from the dining area, and barely larger than those you find on airplanes. In an alcove was a washbasin and a door that led to the outside storage area, mainly used for empty crates and bottles and for washing and peeling vegetables.

I staked a claim to the small table between the kitchen area and the refrigerated display units and set up my food processor and work area there. Since Mémis was apparently also going to help (at no extra cost, it seemed) and had clearly fallen for the potato cutter, I left it for him to find a place for it.

❋

On Friday evening Theológos had returned from Athens laden with supplies for the initial summer siege, his fingers bristling, like a tout at the racetrack, with all manner of handwritten receipts, most as incomprehensible as the figures he had presented me with the previous Monday.

Nevertheless, to demonstrate that I wasn't as gullible as I often seemed (and actually was), I sat down with him and assiduously went over every receipt, checking them against the items he had brought back with him and adding up the amounts. Not only did everything tally, but his estimate had been astonishingly on the nose—just a little over thirty thousand drachmas including, as he had said, his boat ticket and hotel room.

Also, the supplies he had brought would last a long while, and some of them were precious, particularly the packages of frozen filet mignon, a delicacy nearly unknown on the island and as yet never offered in one of its restaurants. In fact, the filet mignon, as Steak au Poivre (page 222), would be one of the two centerpieces of the meal I was making for my Norwegian friends, the other being Chicken Retsina (page 224), a dish I had first concocted at a friend's on Mykonos when the cupboard was bare save for a chicken in the freezer, grapes hanging on a trellis over the door, and a large, wicker-covered bottle of retsina in the pantry.

On Saturday morning, Magnus telephoned to say that he and the others, who now numbered twelve, including a couple of Greek friends, were coming at about eight. Later that afternoon, as soon as the meager luncheon crowd had dispersed, I began preparing dinner.

At the same time, of course, I had to wedge myself into the tavérna's established routines, working around and sometimes barging through all the usual things that Démetra and the kids had been doing from time immemorial to get the tavérna ready for dinner.

I also had to put up with helpful hints and innumerable questions on the order of, "We usually chop the garlic with a knife" and "You're going to put grapes in the chicken?!"

The evening, however, was a great success. For the customers anyway. And, initially, for me. Danielle and the children joined us, as did many others who had either heard about the gathering during the day or happened upon it as they came in search of food. All in all, we served about thirty people, which must have broken a record for Livádi at that time of year, when there were very few people as yet vacationing in the valley and no way to get there except by taxi or by covering the five miles from the port on foot.

Everyone loved the food and kept up such a constant stream of orders that my plans to sit down and play the host—the pasha in residence, à la Theológos—were continually frustrated. He, on the other hand, having left the limelight to me, hobnobbed to his heart's content.

Though much of what happened remains a blur, the pivotal point of the evening—my first lesson of the season—stands out to this day with terrible clarity.

I was passing the long table where Magnus and his group were eating and drinking with noisy gusto. One of that group was a Patmian from Skála, Chrístos, a longtime friend of both Magnus's and mine, the man, in fact, who had first directed me to Hóra the day I arrived on the island. He called out my name, and, as there happened to be an empty chair next to him, I was gratefully moving to sit down for a moment when he abruptly held up a plate of *tzatzíki* and said, "What is this?"

I looked down at the creamy mixture of yogurt, oil, cucumber, and garlic. In it was a large, greenish fly, quite dead. The situation so resembled a *New Yorker* cartoon that I almost laughed.

"Chrísto," I said, "I'm sorry!"

Instead of an understanding shrug, which would have let me off the hook, Chrístos's expression remained as flat as a piece of shale. And in a voice equally as flat, he said, "Thomá, this is not the way you run a restaurant."

At that moment, I understood exactly which side of the fence I was now on. I was no longer a friend or an equal, or even a tourist. Nor even simply a taker. I was a servant. And even though I could be as chummy as I wanted, it was incumbent upon me to never, ever, forget the reality of the situation or my place in it. This wasn't one of my dinner parties, not under any circumstances, no matter how much I wanted it to be.

※

The second lesson came several days later when Theológos and I were doing our accounts so I could pay him the money I owed for the supplies he had bought in Athens.

We began totaling up the week's receipts, but instead of starting with the big money maker on Saturday, Theológos said, "Okay, Monday—"

"What about Saturday?" I asked.

He looked genuinely surprised.

"We must have made a lot of money," I continued.

"We?" he said. "But you said you wanted to cook for your friends."

"Yes." A small, very cold ball was beginning to form in the center of my stomach.

"So I made you a favor."

"Yes?"

"But our contract says you began Monday. The fifteenth. That's what we agreed on."

"Then why do you think I worked on Sunday, too?"

Theológos shrugged. "I thought you liked to help."

"Theológo—"

"A contract is a contract, Thomá. You know that better than anybody. You're an American."

I couldn't even speak. Meanwhile, he looked at my tortured face, a pained expression of disappointment on his own, as if he had been expecting better of me. Then he said, "I'm sorry you thought something else."

God's word.

Comfort Food

I briefly considered quitting. But then how would I have gotten my investment back—by going to the Greek police? Sure.

Of course, it wasn't really the money that was at stake. It was my pride, my insistence that in spite of the facts, I could still turn a sow's ear into a silk purse. Did I really expect I could take a way of doing things that was at least two thousand years old and turn it around in a couple of days into a model of integrity? Only by being honest myself?

But just because Theológos had pulled this little stunt, was I going to turn tail and run? And then expose myself to all those "I-told-you-so's" from people like Melyá? Not to mention Danielle.

No. My dream was at stake, and I wasn't going to let anybody take it from me, particularly not Theológos with his petty need to gyp me out of the relatively few drachmas we had made on Saturday night.

Besides, he was teaching me a valuable lesson. A little brutal, perhaps, but that's life. So, I thought, okay, lesson learned. That's the last time he's going to do this to me.

I got up from the table where we'd been sitting and went back to the kitchen—where I prepared my initial batch of Chili con Carne (page 216) as comfort food, perhaps, and to prove that I was still my own man.

As it happened, the first customers for lunch that day were a girl and a boy from California, eighteen at the most, dusty backpackers who had wandered out to Livádi in search of a remote beach to camp on.

I took them to the display case and the kitchen to show them what we had ready, not even mentioning the chili, thinking that this was the last thing they'd be interested in. But it was on the stove simmering, and they caught the aroma.

"What's that?" asked the girl.

"Oh," I replied, dismissively, "that's just some chili I made up. Now this moussaka—"

"Chili?" said the boy. "You mean, like, chili con carne?"

"Yeah. I thought I'd try it. But this moussaka I made—"

The boy and girl looked at each other. "Isn't that cool?!" they said. "Chili in Greece?!" They turned to me. "Can we have some?" asked the boy.

"You want chili?"

"Yeah," he said. "You don't know what it's been like, backpacking around for weeks, eating nothing but gyros and moussaka and all that stuff—"

The girl, who had hardly taken her eyes off the pot, said, "But chili! Oh my God!" And looked at me as if I had just turned up in the desert with a gallon of ice water.

I gave the order to Démetra, who raised her eyebrows in surprise and then filled two individual earthenware casseroles for me to take out to the kids from California.

Other customers drifted in, and I forgot about the couple. Suddenly they showed up behind me, bowls in hand.

"Could we have some more?" asked the girl.

I was nearly speechless.

"It's really good," said the boy.

"Paradise!" said the girl.

I looked over at Démetra, who happened to be watching. As was Theológos, who'd just wandered in.

"They want some more," I said in Greek. "They think it's wonderful. *Parádiso!*" Then I turned to the boy and girl. "Sure you can have some more. But you have to pay for it, you know?"

"Oh, sure!" they said, bowls held out like supplicants.

Well, not only did they want second helpings, they also had thirds, and by the time lunch was over, even Theológos had tasted the chili. While he may not have had a whole bowl—"It burns!" he said—what he and the others did have to swallow, for a change, was their pride.

In fact, on his next trip to Athens, Theológos, without my asking, returned with two twenty-pound sacks of kidney beans. Definitely comfort food.

Twenty, Twenty-four Seven

In years past, my favorite time of day had always been late afternoon until sunset. At four, people would began leaving the beach, so by five, it was almost entirely deserted. With the sun low in the sky behind the tavérna, the shadows of the tamarisk trees would lengthen across the beach, reaching out toward the sea, whose metallic-blue surface was gradually taking on the changing hues of the sky. If there were clouds to reflect the rays of the setting sun, the effect was magical, particularly with the wind dropping as it usually did in the evening. Then the surface of the sea would seem to float above itself on nearly imperceptible swells, iridescent with contrasting layers and swirls of turquoise, violet, and pink. That there could be such beauty—and such stillness—was almost incomprehensible.

For those of us in the restaurant business, however, this period was incontestably the most anxiety-ridden of the day—the calm before the storm—in which you frantically raced against the clock to clear away the debris of lunch while simultaneously trying to prepare dinner. And if someone wandered in before you were ready, demanding something to eat, it was all you could do not to throttle him on the spot and dump his body out back with the potato peelings. And then fling yourself back into cooking.

In a tavérna like The Beautiful Helen, which also served as the only available café on the beach, you considered yourself lucky if you only had to work eighteen straight hours out of twenty-four. Usually, especially after the height of the season kicked in precisely on July 1, it was twenty out of twenty-four.

The day began at about 7 A.M. when coffee and some form of breakfast had to be served both to the local fishermen returning from their nocturnal sea prowls and the early risers among the noncarousing (or sometimes, still drunk) vacationers.

During that same period, the main meals of the day from stove-topped stews to baked items such as moussaka and stuffed tomatoes and peppers had to be started. In addition, as many bowls of salad as the refrigerator could hold were assembled in advance, as well as dips like *tzatzíki* (Yogurt, Cucumber, and Garlic Dip, page 206) and *melitzánosaláta* (Eggplant Dip, page 208).

Démetra would make most of the basic Greek items with ruthless efficiency, hacking up her ingredients by the bunch and then seeming to measure them solely according to how much she managed to grab in one hand before tossing whatever it was into boiling water or sizzling oil.

I, on the other hand, would place my cookbook on a little stand I had brought for the purpose and carefully measure out everything spoon by spoon and cup by cup. Sometimes I would catch Démetra, in the midst of her whirlwind, looking at me out of the corner of an eye sparkling with amusement, her gold tooth glinting. But she had to admit that the dishes I fixed were tasty—although she never ate a whole meal of any of them. Except the moussaka, which she thought was wonderful and helped me prepare with considerable deference.

Lunch lasted from about eleven until three or four, at which time—while the rest of the civilized world was either napping or making love or taking showers and getting dressed for cocktails and the social whirl of the evening—those of us who slaved in restaurants would have to clean up the mess they had made at lunch and then begin to prepare their repast for the evening.

In Greece in the summer, dinner begins at about seven, heats up at eight, and really goes into full swing between nine and ten. After that, depending upon the makeup of the crowd and whether or not *kéfi* has descended, a full-fledged party may set in. If it does, the evening can be prolonged until well after midnight, sometimes until 3 or 4 A.M. Afterward, the restaurant has to be cleaned and the dishes and glasses and pots and pans washed, and the refrigerator refilled with wines, beers, water, and soft drinks. And after that—seemingly about ten minutes later—you've got to get up again at six-thirty to start the day all over.

People have asked me why we didn't just tell our customers to leave earlier and close the tavérna about midnight. Or conversely, why we didn't just not open for breakfast. Or both. Well, believe it or not, aside from the considerable amount of money to be made at night—the profit margin on drinks is about 80 percent, as opposed to perhaps 10 percent on food— you also feel a great sense of obligation to your customers, many of whom show up late or in the early morning so piteously grateful to see you open that you don't have the heart to say no either to a request for one last glass of wine or that first cup of the day's coffee.

Since I myself had been guilty many times over the years of keeping the tavérna open until some ungodly hour in the morning—or had gone there straight from all-night parties at friends' houses to beg for breakfast—I was not only well acquainted with the hours a customer like me would make me keep, but was living in a glass house so obviously fragile that I couldn't toss a pebble, much less a stone.

So, as the days lengthened into weeks and the gentle, civilized sanity of June was suddenly shattered on July 1 by hordes of invaders from the north, my recollections melt into the kind of frenetic, unrecapturable blur that is similar, I imagine, to the experience of soldiers in the heat of battle.

Inside the citadel of The Beautiful Helen, it seemed to me that we had suddenly become the Trojans, and outside, camped on the beach, were the besieging Greeks and their allies, tranquilly beginning their day with a swim and some sunbathing before rising from their encampments to throw themselves at us in wave after endless wave throughout the day and sometimes far into the night.

In the beginning, pride and adrenaline rushes drove me on. Being in the heat of things was exhilarating, and I wasn't going to let Démetra and those two little boys, not to mention young

Mémis—who was now having a fling with Lili—outwork me and, moreover, shame me in front of Theológos.

In addition, there were always enough compliments from the customers to keep the energy flowing.

Imagine what it's like when a party of fifteen from France calls you over during lunch and asks if they can reserve a table for themselves again that night and gives you carte blanche to make them whatever you want? France?! That afternoon, I did everything I could to create something truly special for the evening, a meal of two complementary chicken dinners that would be far from the normal run of French or Western cooking—a Chinese dish whose distinctive feature was the last minute smothering of the chicken with thinly sliced cucumbers (Chinese Chicken with Cucumbers, page 228); and one of my Indian favorites, a Murghi (or Mughlai) curry with yogurt, almonds, and raisins (Curried Chicken, page 230).

At the end of the meal, I recall the elegant young woman who seemed to be the leader of the group coming up to me in the kitchen to thank me. She was about twenty, with a pale oval face framed by long, straight dark hair, her eyes a sparkling dark brown, a beauty mark perfectly placed at the corner of her smile. "We have to leave tomorrow," she said, "and I am so sorry that I didn't know about your restaurant until now. But—" She smiled again and held out her hand for mine. "Perhaps next year?"

I was giddy for the next two days.

While money was pouring in, however, it was also pouring out in such a steady stream that we never seemed to get enough ahead to pocket anything more than the weekly salary we had allotted ourselves in our initial agreement—ten thousand drachmas for Theológos and myself, and considerably less for Démetra and the boys. There were always more supplies to buy, both as replacements for what we had used and, in the drink department, to stockpile against the inevitable drought of August, when distributors on the mainland would all but cut us off.

Every day or two, Theológos would return from the market in Skála with a new batch of those unreadable receipts for me to add up, and after a while, exhausted and always in the middle of preparing lunch, I began to dismiss them with a wave of my hand. He would pat me on the back as I bent over my chopping block and say, "Don't worry, Thomá. The *paneyíri* is coming."

The *paneyíri* he was talking about was the major religious festival of the year for Livádi. Held on August 6, it was celebrated throughout Greece, but most particularly in those communities that had a church consecrated to the Transfiguration of Christ, in Greek, *ee Metamórfosi*—the Metamorphosis.

In Livádi, the Church of the Transfiguration was tiny, little more than a chapel and barely large enough for a priest and perhaps ten other people. Nor was there sufficient land outside to hold any sort of celebration. Therefore, the staging of the feast itself, always occurring on the evening before, had long ago been given over to the cafés in Upper Livádi and The Beautiful Helen on the beach. For these establishments, it was the traditional turning point of the summer, the day on which all their previous hard work paid off and the money tree at last bore fruit.

I was assured, not only by Theológos but by the two café owners in Upper Livádi, that on that night we would take in enough money to recoup all of our previous expenses and make much of the rest of the summer nothing but pure profit.

Also, the *paneyíri* party on the eve of August 6 would mark the ninth anniversary of the night when Danielle and I had first made love. Since it was beginning to feel as though nine more years had passed since the last time we had gotten together for this particular purpose, the coming event was beginning to take on much added significance.

If I have not mentioned Danielle and the children recently, this is because they, too, like life at the tavérna, were becoming a kind of blur. I would glimpse them as they passed by on their way to the beach or watched forlornly from a distant table as I rushed back and forth from the kitchen, barely even having time to take their order.

Sometimes Sara would try to follow me into the kitchen to help, as she had been doing back home in Rethymnon, but she would inevitably become tangled up in the incessant swirl that went on between the kitchen and the dining area, Sávas, Lámbros, and myself serving, Démetra and Mémis cooking, chopping, and cleaning. And then poor little two-year-old Matt would come trundling in, stark naked, to find his sister and his father, arms raised in a happy anticipation of a hug. Instead, what he got was me sweeping him off the floor and depositing him on his mother's lap, while Sara, chastened by not being able to keep up with me, would return to stand by her mother's side and gaze up at me wide-eyed and confused.

At night when I came home, they were always asleep. In the morning, the 6:30 A.M. alarm would briefly awaken Danielle, who would mutter, *"Bonjour. Ça va?"* and then immediately sink back into the arms of Morpheus.

In a corner of the bedroom, the table where she worked on her paintings was beginning to resemble the one back in Rethymnon, fecund with brushes, jars, bottles, tubes, and a stack of worm-eaten wood, while on the floor, leaning against the walls, were a series of elaborately painted icons, all in various stages of completion, their gold surfaces gleaming softly in the sunlight seeping in around the edges of the wooden shutters.

Before going out on the terrace, I would peek in at the chil-

dren in their beds in the middle room. Sara was always so perfectly covered by her sheet that it looked as if she had not
moved a millimeter since she had turned on her side to sleep,
her shoulder-length blond hair, now nearly white from the sun
and sea salt, streaking her cheeks and pillow. Matt, pacifier in
his mouth and salt-encrusted hair as spiky as a punk rocker's,
always looked as though he had gone a good fifteen rounds
with his bedclothes, and was so tangled in coiled sheets that
covering him up again was beyond possibility.

Their room, meanwhile, had become a repository for more
junk than Theológos's walk-in refrigerator. Aside from the
books and various toys that we had brought with us, mementos
of their days littered the floor and windowsill—pebbles, rocks,
bits of colored glass, bottles filled with sand, seashells of all
kinds, bits of fishermen's nets and the corks that were used to
float them, the chalky skeletons of squid, twisted stumps of
driftwood, pottery shards, bottle tops, and starfish husks. Like
Danielle, they had put their markings on the house and made it
a home.

Since it was almost impossible to go through their room
without stepping on something, I would slip out onto the terrace to go around to the kitchen. There I would have a quick
cup of coffee and an even quicker bath, this accomplished by
standing in a plastic washtub as I poured barely warmed water
over myself from a pot heated on our two-burner stove.

But this little torture was next to nothing compared to the
daily heart-wrench I would suffer when I returned to the terrace and had to face in the opposite direction. Then, I would be
unable to avoid looking across the valley at the whitewashed
form of Comnénus, the farmhouse we had bought shortly
before Sara's birth, nestled in clusters of bougainvillea and
carob and pine trees and bathed in the misted amber glow of
the early morning sun.

It had been this same sight, morning after morning seven years before, which had one day caused me to turn to Danielle, only just pregnant with Sara, and say, "You know what? We're going to buy that place."

Comnénus

At the end of our first summer on the island, neither Danielle nor I had intended to stay on much past August, but once we had found each other, it seemed an excellent idea to linger at least through the glorious days of September. And then maybe through October. . . .

In late September, at my persistent urging, she moved in with me into the house on the hill. A week or so later, I received a telegram from my agents in New York announcing that they had sold my novel and had gotten me an advance of five thousand dollars.

Suddenly, I had become a writer.

And just as suddenly, it seemed that I did not have to hurry back anywhere.

So I began a campaign to persuade Danielle to spend the winter on Patmos, where we would do nothing but write and paint and walk the hills and the seashores and make love.

As I said earlier, fateful things seem to happen to you in Greece, more than in other places. And these lead to other things, and others, and before you know it, a soft, velvet chain of circumstance has quietly wound itself around you. And one day, if all is going well, as it was with us, you find yourself saying, in full concert with the Greeks, *"O tee théli O Theh-óhs!"* "Whatever God wants!"

First, the news about the novel had arrived at exactly the right moment, just as my money for the summer was running disturbingly low. In January, the stock market started to take off, and in the halcyon days that followed (a Greek term, by the way, for an Indian summer that occurs in the month after Christmas), I found myself basking shirtless on our terrace reading the financial pages of my newly subscribed to airmail edition of the *International Herald Tribune* and calculating that while it was costing me perhaps five dollars a day to live in Livádi, my initial ten-thousand-dollar investment was piling up and sometimes making close to five hundred dollars for the same twenty-four-hour period on the New York Stock Exchange.

The trend continued that summer, and so, in August, when we learned that Danielle was pregnant, it took us all of a minute to decide to have the baby.

We were on a roll, in love, and flush with the knowledge that while tourists on Patmos were returning to their jobs in the real world, we were staying on in Livádi to live the kind of life they could only dream about. And not only that. We had money. Not a lot, but more than enough to manage.

Thus, everything, including her pregnancy, was just as it should be.

The change in Danielle was remarkable. When we had first started living together, she had been model-slim and plagued by a family susceptibility to asthma, which, when it struck, left her frighteningly gaunt. With her pregnancy, however, the asthma attacks gradually lessened in severity and then vanished. Now, her cheeks were plump and glowing, and she was even at times taking over the kitchen to cook the kinds of meals her mother used to make, thrown together in that casually efficient manner of a French *maman* of five, and absolutely delicious.

So there I was, a father-to-be, waking up every morning and looking across the valley at this abandoned two-story farmhouse, while the value of my stake in the market gradually rose from $10,000 to $20,000 to $25,000 and then to $35,000, with stock splits and dividends coming right to left, until, when I finally pulled out altogether that winter (at just the right time, it turned out), I had almost $40,000 to play with.

When I told Danielle I wanted to try and buy the house, she was already so impressed by my financial acumen (which I suspected was pure luck) that she just sat there on the terrace, perhaps a little stunned at the craziness of the idea, and said, "Whatever you want."

I called Melyá to ask if she'd help, and she immediately leapt on the bandwagon. In fact, since she had already been thinking about getting a place on Patmos herself, it seemed like a perfect arrangement, particularly as the family who owned the farmhouse also had property for sale in Hóra.

The people of Livádi had two names for the property I wanted. It was called the *pírgos,* or tower, because it was then the only two-story structure in the valley, and Comnénus because this was the name of the family that owned it. Descendants of a line of Byzantine emperors who had come to live and prosper in Hóra after the fall of Constantinople (present-day Istanbul) to the Turks in 1453, they had used the house in Livádi for summer vacations. Now, with only a frail and elderly brother and sister still occupying the family mansion in Hóra, it had fallen into near disuse, visited solely by the farmer next door, who paid a modest yearly tithe to work the land.

It would take another book entirely to tell the story of the truly Byzantine negotiations needed to acquire the house from the Comnénus family, which, it turned out, had thirty-five heirs scattered worldwide from Milwaukee to Australia. And then there were the subsequent harrowing experiences that Danielle and I (and little Sara in her womb) went through during the pregnancy. These included a near miscarriage, a bus crash in Athens, a trip to and through Turkey in order to get our expired visas renewed, the near swamping of our hired caïque as we attempted to return to Patmos in a winter storm, and finally, Sara's abrupt arrival a month early. No doubt she decided to abandon her mother's precarious belly as soon as the getting was good.

Once the Comnénus house was ours we had to engage in a pitched battle to make it livable. The workers we hired to fix the roof, upstairs terrace, and walls would show up for perhaps four days in a row and then suddenly evaporate for a month or more, first pleading bad weather, and then, maddeningly, a prior commitment to finish work on someone else's house. The same went for the electricians and plumbers from Skála and the door and window maker from the nearby valley of Kámbos.

So instead of the plan I had formed to bring our new baby back from Athens to the comforts of a freshly renovated seven-room home with hot and cold running water, we were faced with the monstrous task (not so unfamiliar, however, to the people of Livádi) of dealing with a deluge of dirty diapers in the house on the hill, whose water, if you remember, had to be carried up from a well fifty yards below.

The solution I eventually devised for the diaper cleaning problem (should anyone have a need to know) was to affix the rubber suction cup of a toilet plunger to the end of a broom-stick, put soapy water in a black plastic bucket to heat up on the sun-blasted terrace, and wash the diapers every time we went past by giving the plunger a few quick ups and downs. Of course, in the winter the water never got very hot, but you did have the occasional compensation of rain to do the rinsing for you. . . .

But there was always the daily satisfaction, once these chores were finished and the roof of the Comnénus house was in place, of going over to work on its interior, staining the beamed ceilings, cleaning and polishing the hundred-year-old red-brick tiles that covered the downstairs floors, and burrowing into the countless other tiny, immensely satisfying tasks that go into making a house a home.

Meanwhile, back at the house on the hill, Danielle and I celebrated our first undisturbed candlelight dinner since Sara's birth with a meal I christened Spaghetti Sara Sleeping (page 242) in honor of the fact that she slept through the entire meal, a miraculous event. Once again, it used whatever was at hand, in this case, a supply of dried black Chinese mushrooms sent to us by Danielle's mother, zucchini, garlic, evaporated milk, and spaghetti.

At about the same time, another meal marked the end of a continuing standoff I had been having with Stélios and Varvára's rooster.

The tale of this confrontation is so eerily similar to one recounted in Peter Mayle's wonderful memoir *A Year in Provence,* that I can't resist telling it here both as an example of the kind of life we were then living and as proof that there really is a Jungian collective unconscious—at least as far as it concerns alpha males among men and roosters, their poultry counterparts.

In honor of another writer whose work I deeply admire, M. F. K. Fisher,* I have called the story:

How to Cook a Rooster

He had been there ruling his territory long before the day I first made my tortuous way over Livádi's rock-strewn fields and bramble-covered walls to see if the house was for rent.

His domain was the entire area around the house on the hill, front and back. With his harem of about fifteen

---

*See her marvelous wartime book, *How to Cook a Wolf,* for the ways in which she dealt with shortages similar to the ones we would endure annually during Lent on Patmos.

hens, he would spend the day—from about 4 A.M. to sunset—free-ranging over the bluff and back into the huge patch of cacti to the rear, where the hens would often lay their eggs.

We had never liked each other.

First of all, as soon as rosy-fingered dawn even hinted at an approach, the rooster would launch his first caws of the day, a well-honed, mounting series of squawks that penetrated my inch-thick shutters with the ease and impact of a medieval battle-ax.

In the beginning, I had thought this was quaint, having a real rooster living right outside the house. But that was in the early days when I was working monklike on my novel and going to bed and rising with the sun anyway.

After Danielle entered my life, however, my outlook on many things radically changed—especially with regards to getting to sleep (but not to bed) early.

So one night that August, when we'd been out on the town for more than a few drinks and had come back to the house well after midnight, we had just dozed off (it seemed) when suddenly the rooster let loose with an onslaught of screeches that topped any I had ever heard before. I sat bolt upright and peered at the bedside clock. Three A.M. An hour before dawn.

When the rooster fired another barrage as horrific as the first, I leapt over the top of a startled Danielle and crashed through the door to the terrace.

Outside it was pitch black. Not even a hint of dawn. As I had suspected, this vicious attack had been entirely unprovoked and was a deliberate attempt on the part of the rooster to ruin my sleep.

In the darkness, I groped for and found one of the heavy rocks that I used for propping open the bedroom doors against the wind.

The rooster crowed again—in every sense of the word—knowing that he had not only awakened me but had brought me out to the terrace totally naked and in a state of possibly fatal apoplexy.

Danielle joined me just as I launched the rock in the direction of his third full-throated caw and, to my horror, heard the cry instantly cut off at its highest pitch.

There was a moment of deathly silence.

Out of the darkness came the excited, concerned clucking of the beast's retinue. But not a peep from him.

Danielle took hold of my hand, and we pressed against each other in the night, naked and quivering with guilt.

"Do you think . . . ?" she whispered.

"I don't know."

The following morning, we remained huddled in the shuttered darkness of our house, terrified to face Stélios and Varvára. But we couldn't wait forever. Nature was calling, and our toilet was outside at the end of the terrace. I cautiously opened the door and peeked out to see if anyone was around.

There, strutting among his entourage, was the rooster, happily pecking away as if this were a day like any other. He lifted his head when I emerged—and fixed me with a flinty glare. He knew.

Several days later, when I was able to joke about it, I told Stélios and Varvára the story. They laughed. I said, "Do me a favor. One day, if you ever kill the rooster, let me know."

"Why?" they asked.

"Because I want to eat him."

Stélios broke into a wide, understanding grin.

Time passed.

About a year and a half later, when I was on my way home from working on the Comnénus house, Varvára called out to me. She was standing in the door of their kitchen-bedroom. Stélios was behind her. In Varvára's hands was a bowl of soup. She was always giving us things to eat, so I didn't think much of it. I thanked her and took the bowl.

"Umm!" I said, looking at it, "chicken soup!"

They both stood there grinning, their smiles widening by the second.

"What?" I asked.

"*O petinós sou!*" said Stélios. "Your rooster!"

I had won. Or at least, thought I had.

The soup turned out to be tasty, but nowhere near as satisfying as I had once hoped. For one thing, after all those years of free-ranging, the flesh on the rooster's leg was about as chewable as that of a retired soccer player. Second, I had to admit that when all was said and done, he had been a noble antagonist, full of integrity as far as his life's work was concerned, a true cock-of-the-walk. And third, I had noticed, while I was eating the soup, that his successor, young and vigorous, was already out there on the job.

So, in the grand scheme of things, there was really very little for me to crow about.

The End of Comnénus

Shortly after we moved into the Comnénus house, my luck began to change for the worse. This may or may not have been due to the posthumous revenge of the rooster or, more likely, to the sudden appearance of a elderly woman at our gate on the very day we were moving in, a bright October morning some eighteen months later than our builders had sworn the house would be ready.

She was in her sixties or seventies and wore a black, broad-rimmed tulle hat, an elegant black suit that could have been a Chanel, a double string of pearls around her neck, and a considerable amount of jewelry on her fingers and wrists. Her face was lightly powdered, her watery blue eyes ringed with kohl, and her lips thick with a wide slash of red lipstick. But there was considerable dignity in the way she held herself and moved her hands, a posture and presence that spoke of early training in the best salons and finishing schools.

Accompanying her was an extremely embarrassed Evripídes, who had brought her out to the beach in his taxi and then been forced to lead her up the riverbed to our house, all the while, no doubt, having to listen to the long list of grievances that she would soon all but nail on our door. His fisherman's cap, never off his head as long as I could remember, was now clutched obeisantly in his hand, exposing a vulnerable, shiny, bald pate ringed with graying hair.

I saw them approach as I was standing in the kitchen and went out onto the path from the gate to meet them. I said hello in Greek. She replied in thickly accented but perfect French.

"I am Madame Busset," she announced. "You are on my property!"

"Pardon?" I replied, looking around for help. But Danielle was a good one hundred very rocky yards away, back with Sara inside the house on the hill, packing.

"You are on my property!" she repeated, looking over my shoulder at the house.

Suddenly, I realized who she was. A distant cousin of the Comnénus family, several times removed, who had come into a share of the property when another, closer cousin from Egypt had died in the course of our researching the title to the land. She had been the only one of the final thirty-five heirs who had refused to sign the papers transferring the deed to Melyá. Our lawyers assured us that her threat to the ownership was nonexistent, and so we forgot about her.

Apparently, however, she wasn't going to go away that easily. Like the rooster.

On the other hand, she was one of those people who come at you so spoiling for a fight that they are easily disarmed by being treated with absolute deference.

"Ah!" I said, recovering from the initial shock. "You are Madame Busset! I am so happy at last to meet you! Won't you come in and have some coffee?"

Her startled eyes opened wide for a moment, then quickly rehooded themselves.

"*Non!*" She marched past me and around to the terrace at the front of the house. Evripídes and I followed in her wake, both of us quickly reduced to the role of lackeys, he mumbling apologies to me under his breath: "*I didn't know who she was, Thomá, I swear!*"

Madame Busset paused for a moment on the terrace, looking out across the fields to the sea sparkling in the morning sun some three hundred yards away. Then she stepped out into the garden, to the well that sat under a row of tall fir trees. Again she paused and looked out.

As I approached, she said, "I used to come here as a little girl."

I waited for a long while for her to continue, but that was all she had to say.

I asked if I could get her a chair.

She turned toward me, gaze softening slightly. "Yes," she said, "thank you."

Eventually, she also permitted me to bring her coffee, but

steadfastly refused to go into the house. That part of the property was mine, she said. This part, under the fir trees and next to the well, was hers.

Eventually, Danielle, who had looked over from the terrace of the other house and seen this strange figure in black sitting upright on a chair in the garden sipping coffee, came to find out what in God's name was going on.

Most of the time, she and Sara and I watched Madame Busset from behind the shadows of the downstairs window screens as she remained in place—an hour at least—musing under the trees while Evripídes stood respectfully behind her like the servant she must have imagined him to be.

As I served more coffee and later brought Danielle and Sara out to meet her, we learned bits and pieces of her past—that she had grown up in Egypt and been married at seventeen to a young Egyptian-Greek physician; that her husband had succumbed to cancer after being dispossessed by Nasser's revolution; and that now she was living childless and alone on Rhodes in a tiny apartment amid her memories and the few trinkets she had been allowed to take with her out of Egypt.

She cherished the memory of visiting Comnénus one summer long ago when she was a little girl. She had been dressed in a white frock, she said, and a hat with a pink ribbon. . . .

It was clear without her explicitly saying so that she would never, ever, give up her portion of this link to her childhood and her Byzantine heritage.

Abruptly, she stood up and announced that she was taking her leave. She thanked me for the coffee and turned to Danielle. *"Enchanté,"* she said. She touched one-year-old Sara, clinging to my pants leg, on the head, and looked up at me.

"I will speak with my lawyers," she announced.

She then marched imperiously down the path and through the gate, Evripídes following.

For months, we waited for the other shoe to drop, but we never heard from her again. Unless, of course, it was her envy—she had the requisite blue eyes—which consciously or unconsciously set the power of the *kakó máhti*, the evil eye, into motion and produced the string of bad luck that followed.

First there was the investment I made in a Greek freighter. Seduced by the success I had had in the stock market and figuring I couldn't make a mistake, I had asked Melyá if a ship-owning cousin would let me invest ten thousand dollars in one of his vessels. The cousin, a resident of London and a true gentleman, agreed to accept my pittance. Within weeks, the freighter business became mired in a slump that, for all I know, it may still be in. Two years later, the cousin, after returning half my money to me, was forced to tell his other shareholders that he was declaring bankruptcy.

Meanwhile, I had put what was left of the rest of my capital back in the stock market, but it continued to go down. We had been able to buy the Comnénus house for seven thousand dollars, and the restoration—a new roof and windows, running water and electricity—had cost about three thousand. After the expenses of having the baby, we still had about ten thousand. But it was no longer enough to make us feel comfortable.

On the other hand, now that we were at last living in the luxury of Comnénus, little else mattered. We were surrounded by a virtual Garden of Eden, rich with vineyards and carob, pear, almond, fig, and olive trees, wild oregano, rosemary, and thyme, and the wealth of seasonal vegetables planted by the farmer next door.

Unless you've experienced it, you can't imagine the delicious satisfaction of eating your own tomatoes hot off the vine, or the incredible delicacy of new potatoes boiled within minutes of their having been unearthed just outside your kitchen door. Nor are there many people who have enjoyed, as I did, the glorious intoxication of making their own wine by stomping around barefoot, calf- and ankle-deep, in a huge concrete tub filled with grapes from their own vineyard.

It was unthinkable that we would ever have to give this up.

And then came that moment when were emptying our coin jar to gather together enough money to get back to Rethymnon, and we knew, without a doubt, that the idyll was over.

So here we were, in this summer of my Greek tavérna, back in the old house on the hill, gazing like Madame Busset at a landscape of memories, of phantoms, while Comnénus sat as abandoned as I had first seen it, its doors locked and windows shuttered, the Dutch owners as yet undecided about whether or not they had either the time or the desire to make it to Patmos that year.

Had our loss of Comnénus been a result of Madame Busset's envy? There was no way of knowing—just as there would be no way of finding out who was responsible for the trouble I was about to encounter down at The Beautiful Helen.

Toh Kakó Máhti

For a while, all my wildest fantasies about the tavérna had seemed to be coming true.

It turned out that a woman who had been eating regularly at the tavérna during the last week of June was a correspondent for an Athens English-language newspaper. At the beginning of July, she published an article with photographs of Patmos and the tavérna, giving The Beautiful Helen a glowing review and writing about the American who was running it.

So, in addition to the normal crowds that came with the start of the summer season, there was a significant number of customers dropping by because of the article.

I was ecstatic. And even beginning to have daydreams of

buying Comnénus back. My Greek friends, on the other hand, with their customary respect for the power of envy and the way it provoked the evil eye, would just glance at the article and photo and then change the subject. I smiled, glad that I wasn't letting such silly superstitions lead me around by the nose.

The police came looking for me at the end of the first week of July.

It was a Sunday lunch, and we were packed with customers. As it happened, I was standing in full view serving a roadside table when their car came to a stop opposite me.

"Yásoo!" I said, grandly greeting them while still holding plates in both my hands.

The two cops opened their respective doors and stepped out, aviator glasses glinting darkly in the noonday sun. In spite of the heat, they were in full uniformed regalia, jacket and ties, lacking only leather-holstered pistols to make the picture complete.

On most Greek islands, the police are very friendly, often becoming such an intimate part of the community that they are regularly rotated to other islands to avoid their losing their objectivity, through friendship and/or, to put it delicately, financial involvement. So the appearance of the police here or at any other restaurant was nothing unusual—where else were they going to eat?—but this was the first time that summer they had shown up at The Beautiful Helen. And it didn't look like they'd come for lunch.

The memory I hold of what followed is exactly the kind you have of an auto accident you've been in, when everything seems to have happened in slow motion and, in going over it in your mind, you can pause time to mull over the little ironies and what-if's of each instance.

"Are you Kírios Sto-oón?" one of them asked in Greek, his plump cheeks sleek from shaving.

"Yes."

"Do you work here?"

"Uh—" I said, the plates I was still holding getting heavier by the second, "—yes."

The other one, with a mustache and bad skin, spoke up. "Do you have a work permit?"

"I do—yes—uh—for the tutoring school that I work in—in Rethymnon?" I said helpfully.

They stared at me.

Theológos arrived and asked what the problem was. There followed a rapid exchange in Greek, a few sentences of which I understood. "But he's just here helping me," was Theológos's main point. "Only today. We have a lot of customers."

"He has to stop," said the mustache.

"For years I have helped him," I said. "Every summer."

"You have to stop," said the mustache.

"Just let me finish serving these people," I pleaded, holding out the plates.

"You have to stop. Now."

"But . . ."

Theológos took the plates.

The other cop said, "You will come to see the chief of police in Skála tomorrow morning at nine o'clock. With your passport and your Residence Permit. And that work permit from Rethymnon."

After they left, I quickly went inside the tavérna, away from the curious stares of everyone who had witnessed this spectacle, this humiliation. Theológos sat down with me a little later, as did Danielle and the children, innocently arriving from the beach. And after the lunch period was over, others came to commiserate—Démetra and the boys, and some friends from the valley and from Skála and Hóra.

There were all kinds of theories. I wondered if it might have been because of the article. The others thought it was someone in Skála, probably a restaurant owner. Danielle agreed.

"They don't like a foreigner taking away their business," she said.

"But I don't have any enemies in Skála!" I replied. "They've been our friends for years!"

Danielle smiled in that knowing way the French have and shrugged.

"It's not enemies," said a deep voice. "It's the goddamn evil eye!"

I turned around. It was Lili from Norway, her flaming curls concealed under a white terry-cloth hood, blue eyes peering over a pair of tinted, gold-rimmed Armani spectacles. Beside her was Mémis, his usual bright smile dimmed by worry about my problem.

"Oh, come on, Lili!" I said.

"The evil eye?!" asked Sara in alarm and looked at Sávas and Lámbros. *"Toh kakó máhti?!"*

"Ko-MAHti!" cried Matt, for whom his big sister had the last word in everything.

As Sávas and Lámbros solemnly nodded, a woman's voice said, "Lili's right."

This was Alíki, an old friend who owned a boutique in Hóra. A Patmian native in her fifties, tanned and buxom, with short-cut blond hair and a husky cigarette voice, she had been a friend since our first summer on Patmos when she had regularly come out to Livádi with her husband, Andréas, an Athenian architect. After his sudden death from a heart attack, Alíki had returned to her family house and opened a shop selling upscale arts and crafts to tourists. Since she had been the one who had finally pushed Danielle and me together at that *paneyíri,* I always listened to what she had to say with a great deal of respect.

But before she could continue, Theológos put his hand on my shoulder and stood up. "I have to work," he said.

"What are we going to do?" I asked, looking up at him as he stood there with that serving towel once again slung over his shoulder.

He shrugged. "Wait to see what the police chief says tomorrow morning."

"Can you talk to him?"

He gave another shrug, the kind the Greeks use when they don't want to go up against the powers that be, head tilted to one side, shoulder lifting slightly, palms upward pleading helplessness.

"What can *I* do?" he asked.

"*Tee tha kánoumeh, Thomá?*" said Démetra. "What can we do?" "*Étsi eénay ee zo-eé!*" she said. "That's how life is!"

"*Nay,*" Mémis chimed in. "*Móno O Theh-óhs kséri!*"

Sávas and Lámbros touched me on the shoulder and followed their father. Back into *my* kitchen.

"What did Mémis say?" asked Lili, sitting next to me in Theológos's chair. After five summers on the island, she was having her first affair with a Greek and had finally taken an interest in the language. So every day or so she had been coming to me for ways of saying certain things to Mémis in Greek, sentences you couldn't find in phrase books, such as, "I love that you don't have any hair on your chest!"

"Mémis said, 'Only God knows,'" I replied.

"God!" she answered. "How helpful!"

"There *is* something you can do," said Alíki, "if it's the evil eye. You can have it taken away."

I looked at her.

"There's a woman in Hóra," she said, "who can perform a— how do you say?—exorcism?"

I looked at Danielle as she barely repressed a smile.

Alíki continued. "I don't think you have any enemies, not real ones, although there may be somebody from Athens, perhaps, who—"

"What about Melyá?" asked Danielle.

Alíki looked surprised. "Melyá? Why Melyá? She's your friend."

"We've . . . had some problems," I said, "but I don't think she would go to the police and . . ."

"Ho, ho!" scoffed Danielle.

Sara stood up. "I'm going to take Matt to the beach," she said, all of six but entrancingly diplomatic. She held out her hand to her little brother. "*Élla,*" she said in the jumbled patois they used between them. "Come. *Viens avec moi.*"

After they left, Alíki said, "Well, I don't know about Melyá—that's your business—but if it is the evil eye, I can call this woman and make an appointment for you. Now. This evening. Before you go to the police chief tomorrow."

"Why not?" said Lili. "I can drive you there and bring you back."

I looked at Danielle. "You want to come?"

"No," she said. "What would we do with the kids?"

Suddenly I recalled Melyá flashing by in her son's Jeep earlier that morning. She had been wearing sunglasses and didn't look toward the tavérna as she passed, but I remembered noticing the tight smile on her lips, thinking how determined she seemed to maintain the breach between us. Now I wondered if that smile might not have been one of anticipation, of knowing what was coming down the pike.

"Okay," I said to Alíki. "Why not?"

✳

The woman in Hóra lived on a dead-end street squeezed against the heavy granite walls of the monastery, her house seeming to grow right out of the bulging rock formation on which the walls were set.

She received us at the thick wooden door that led directly into her kitchen. Alíki made the introductions—the woman's name was Sofía—and then she and Lili went off to wait for me in a nearby café.

Sofía looked so much like Varvára that they might have been sisters—and probably were related in some distant manner the way most Patmians are—with the same broad cheekbones, shining white hair pulled back in a bun, and sparkling, pale blue eyes. But she had almost no wrinkles in her face, and her cheeks were not sunken in the way Varvára's were because of missing teeth. She looked to be in her sixties but could have passed for a prematurely white fifty or so.

As in most of the old houses of Hóra, her kitchen was magnificent, dwarfing its tiny modern appliances. An immense arched stone fireplace with a recessed brick oven took up almost an entire wall. On its wide, waist-high hearth rested a minuscule three-burner stove connected by a rubber hose to a battered gas canister on the floor. Cabinets and glass-front cupboards of richly burnished cedar covered the walls from the brick-tiled floor to the heavy cedar beams supporting the ceiling. A small white refrigerator stood awkwardly near a door, unable to find a place to fit in.

In one corner, part of the rock formation that I had seen outside swelled into the room as if growing there. It was of the same kind of stone that covered the roof of the Grotto of the Apocalypse, the color and contours of a thundercloud, grayish-black and bulbous.

On the other side of the entranceway was a sort of breakfast nook under the room's single, lace-covered window. A silver tray sat on the table. On it were a glass of water and a tiny vial of oil. The only sound came from the ticking of a clock hung on the wall next to the fireplace.

On the drive up to Hóra, Alíki had told Lili and me that the water and oil that the woman used were consecrated in the monastery during its services and then spirited out to Sofía by one of the monks. The church, she said, officially frowned on these sort of exorcisms, while at the same time turning a blind eye to the appropriation of its holy water and oil for the ceremonies. So in case the exorcism worked, the church was ensured a claim in the results.

These rites were held in high esteem by the Greek people and reached far back into the country's prehistory. Individuals with the power to dispel the curse of the evil eye were usually women, and they were addressed not as *Kíria*, Madame, but as *Oseéa*, Blessed.

"So they're kind of priestesses," I had said to Alíki.

"Yes," she replied. "Definitely."

✳

Sofía told me to sit at the table. She asked how I had been feeling lately, and what had happened. I told her. She nodded. Then she made the sign of the cross over my head and muttered a rapid string of words as incomprehensible to me as the receipts that Theológos had brought from the market. Later I would learn that they were a part of the Orthodox liturgy.

Sofía then asked me to take a sip of the holy water. I did so. Next, she held the glass level with my eyes so I could see what was happening and carefully tilted the vial of holy oil over it until a drop of it fell into the water.

It sank straight to the bottom.

Sofía shook her head sadly.

"*T'ókho?*" I asked, hopefully. "I have it?"

She nodded. Then she dipped her finger into the oily water and made the sign of the cross, smooth and cool, on my forehead. Again, she launched into a recitation of some part of the liturgy, much longer this time, at one point rapidly making the sign of the cross over and over in the air between us.

Finally, she held out the glass and told me to drink the water.

"A sip?" I suggested, thinking of the taste of the oil.

She smiled. "All."

✳

Alíki and Lili were waiting for me at the café, a tiny carafe of ouzo and a plate of grilled octopus between them.

"So?"

"She told me to come back in a week."

"Yes," said Alíki. "Then she will drop the oil into the holy water again. If it floats, you're cured."

"Oil *always* floats on water," said Lili.

"No, it doesn't," I replied.

✳

On the drive back to Livádi, Lili wanted to talk about Mémis.

"He's wonderful!" she said. "So sweet! And so direct! None of that negotiating you get from so many men. How do you say— beating around the bush? When he wants you—bang! That's it."

"Bang."

"Yep." As we reached a short straightaway on the serpentine road that wound down from Hóra to Skála, she took her hands off the wheel to insert a cigarette into her long, white holder and just managed to grab the wheel again as a hairpin curve came up.

"He's also very artistic," she continued. "He does collages, driftwood and things."

"Really?"

"Yes." She looked at me accusingly. "When he has the time! You could let him off a little earlier at night, you know."

I was about to argue this point when it suddenly occurred to me how futile this conversation was.

"Lili," I said, "I can't do anything."

※

The next morning I trudged up the hill from our house and caught the eight-thirty bus to Skála. I could have taken the easier route of going down to the beach and picking up the bus or a caïque there, but after Theológos's weak-kneed response of the previous afternoon, I didn't particularly want to see him or The Beautiful Helen again, not on my way to the police station.

The night before, Danielle and I had discussed our options, which seemed to run all the way from zero to one—the one being that if I weren't asked to leave the country because of my transgression, we would immediately head back to Rethymnon. Perhaps I could pick up work at the tutoring school or, worst-case scenario, in Socrátes's restaurant. While I alternated between rage and despair, Danielle was very calm. As she saw it, the main problem would be getting what money we could back from Theológos.

That I hadn't thought of. In fact, I still didn't want to contemplate it. Which was another reason why I hadn't passed by the tavérna on my way to town. I had just as much of an aversion to showdowns as Theológos did.

On the bus I concentrated on what kind of case I could present to the police chief—my love of Patmos and of Greece, my desire to have the children spend the summer in Livádi, where they had been all but born, my deep appreciation of Greek cooking—anything but the main truth, which was that I had been in it for the money.

The police station was—and is—located on the upper floor of the Italianate two-story customs building just off the pier. The bus stop was directly opposite the front door, which I was grateful for, because the shame of yesterday's incident at the tavérna still hung with me, and I didn't want to have to talk about it to anyone in town.

So I quickly slipped into the building and went upstairs. When I entered the outer office, the two cops who were there in their light gray shirts and sharply pressed dark gray trousers turned and looked at me as if I were just another anonymous tourist. "Yes?" they said.

I gave them my name and said the chief wanted to see me. They told me to sit down, and one of them went into the back while the other continued to leaf through a sheaf of papers.

A fan hummed in one corner. The shades on the eastern side had been pulled down to stop the morning sun from flooding in, and the room was suffused with a dim, yellowish light. From the street, the sounds of the growing bustle of Monday morning drifted up—the rattle of motorcycles bouncing by, the chatter of Greeks calling to one another—ordinary goings-on that I suddenly ached to be a part of.

The cop reappeared from the back and said that I should come with him. He led me to a room at the end of the hall and motioned me in.

Much to my surprise, the police chief turned out to be the same one that had been in place before we left for Rethymnon. While we had not exactly been friends, we had spoken on occasion and had several times sat around the same table at restaurants or cafés. He was about my age, maybe a little younger, with dark, neatly trimmed hair graying slightly at the sides and that immaculate, well-fed glow that most Greek police—at least those in the upper ranks—seem to have been born with.

As soon as his subordinate had closed the door and left us alone, he smiled.

"*Tee kánis, Thomá?*" he said. "How are you? And the wife and little girl?"

I told him. And was about to tell him about Matt, too, and my love of Patmos and of Greece and Greek cooking when he went straight to the point.

"You can't work without a permit, Thomá. You know that."

"I know. But always foreigners help in restaurants and shops, and nobody says anything, so I thought—"

"Someone complained."

"Ah!" I waited to hear if he would name names, but he just looked at me and nodded sympathetically, as if he too were appalled at the way people can be.

"So," he said, "what are we going to do?"

He stared at me as if challenging me to come up with a solution. Although this particular chief had an impeccable reputation, later it occurred to me that I should have offered him money. Why didn't I think of this then? I have often been asked that question, because over the years there have been many times when I've been in similar situations and haven't picked up on such a possibility. I don't think that most Americans—ordinary ones—would either. Our minds don't work along those lines. It all goes back to that business with the Cherry Tree, I suppose, which has definitely put most of us at a distinctive disadvantage in the real world.

So I stared back at him.

And, at that moment, I was suddenly struck with an idea so simple and so perfect that it seemed to be nothing less than divine inspiration.

"Can I apply for a restaurant work permit?" I asked.

He paused and then shrugged and said, "Yes. Of course. But they won't give you one."

"But would it be legal for me to work while I'm waiting for their answer?"

He paused again, for a much longer time, and then said, "Yes."

"And how long will it take for an answer to come?"

This time he almost smiled. "From Athens?" he said. "Three or four months . . ."

"October," I said, grinning.

He leaned forward and pressed a button on his intercom. "Kósta! Bring me an application for a work permit!"

He looked up at me and allowed himself the slightest of smiles. As for me, it was all I could do not to throw myself over the desk and smother him in an embrace.

After rushing home to tell Danielle the news, I was back at work in the tavérna before lunch, exultant. Démetra, Mémis, and the boys shared in my delight. A startled Theológos, however, just stared at me, speechless, his entire belief system in shreds. "What did you do?" he asked.

"Nothing," I said. "Just applied for a permit. The chief said I can work while I'm waiting for an answer."

I could tell that he didn't believe me. Such a solution was too simple, too aboveboard. There must have been deeper machinations afoot, bribery, perhaps, or connections in high places.

I was so relieved to be back that I couldn't have cared less what he thought. Nor did I bother to return to Hóra the following week to find out if the curse of the *kakó máhti* had been lifted.

Who had the time?

July

In spite of the heat, and unlike heavy, satiated August, July still has a freshness of anticipation about it, a sense that everything and anything is possible. People start shedding their everyday personas along with their clothes and begin anointing their bodies with oils and lotions, and the air, laced with released perfumes and the subtle tang of sweat, is pungent with promise.

The night after I had been reprieved by the chief of police, Danielle and I made love for the first time in what seemed like weeks. Surviving the attempt to get rid of me—and, in effect, outdoing a Greek at his or her own game—had been like conquering a fatal disease. My appetites were suddenly awakened, refreshed, and life tasted as sweet as it had when I was on the cusp of puberty. Making love with Danielle felt like the old days, eager and abandoned, pulsant with sensuality. For that night, at least, it seemed as if we had at last returned to the real Patmos, the way it had been, back when we had been younger and flush with the intoxications of summer.

I threw myself back into the maelstrom of the tavérna with renewed vigor, heading full sail toward the Transfiguration eve of August 5, the night when everything we had invested was certain to be alchemized into the pure gold of profit. I wasn't just taking people's word for this. I had been to the *paneyíri* for eight straight summers and had seen the crowds and bacchanalian excesses that had engulfed The Beautiful Helen from about eight P.M. until four or five in the morning, stripping it of supplies. This was a guaranteed jackpot, all in one evening.

Meanwhile, money continued to pour in and pour out at an unprecedented rate, so fast and in such quantities that only someone who was above the fray—i.e., sitting day and night at a cash register—could have tracked its movements.

We didn't have the luxury of that, didn't have a register at all, nor were there carbon-papered pads to make copies of the meal checks. Even if we had had the latter, keeping up with the scribbled slips of paper would have been much too time consuming. At the end of the day, at two or three A.M., all you wanted was to fling yourself into bed, while at seven the next morning, contemplating even the lowest forms of mathematics seemed just as much of a torture as it had back in grade school.

During mealtimes, I did my best to tote up the bills for every table myself, but the crush of customers was becoming so overwhelming that I sometimes had to let Sávas and Lámbros do their own calculating. We would make our change out of a cardboard box in a drawer behind the counter and then toss the uncounted profits into it before going on to the next customers. The only bookkeeping we did was with regard to the inviolable tavérna tradition of allowing trusted clientele to run tabs. These would sometimes mount into tens of thousands of drachmas—a regular habit of mine in past summers—and might not be fully paid off until the end of the season. If at all. So you could never know exactly where you stood.

Theológos's stockpiling continued apace, with crates upon crates of beer, wine, and soft drinks rising head-high around the inside walls and central columns, making a trip to find the toilet, for the uninitiated, a definite challenge.

On the worst days, Danielle would try to help, chopping onions, peeling garlic cloves, preparing salads—but it was almost impossible for her to stay for long without both of us worrying about the children. There was no telling what might be happening to them out there in the multiple dangers of the valley, road, beach, and sea, where motorcycles, cars, scorpions, snakes, donkeys, mules, death by drowning, and numerous other hazards lurked in every corner of our imagination.

I remember how startling it sometimes was when Sara or Matt would march up to me in the middle of lunch or dinner and ask for something, these little strangers acting as if they had a special claim on my attention. But there were other times when I would look at them sitting side by side at a table, Sara's hair done up in pigtails, Matt sucking wide-eyed on his pacifier, and could see how proud they were as they watched their papa work his clientele, keeping customers at ten or fifteen different tables happily believing that they and only they were receiving his truly undivided attention.

More and more old friends began to appear, people we had met in summers past who had heard we were back and had come out to see, figuratively and literally, what was cooking. While it was always wonderful to renew acquaintances, it wasn't long before I would have to take their orders, and then the inevitable shift in our relationship would occur. Soon they would be wondering why their food was taking so long to arrive, or where the slice of feta was that they had asked for, or could they *please* get some more water, Tom?

The police came, too, all of them old buddies now, and insisted on paying the check in spite of my efforts to the contrary. Meanwhile, Theológos hung in the background, not yet sure if there was still a possibility of guilt by association.

Magnus and Anna returned the second week of July and moved into the large house that Lili had rented in Livádi to be closer to Mémis. So Lili, Magnus, and Anna became regular customers at the tavérna. In the afternoons, if they were sitting by themselves, Danielle would often join them. Magnus was one of the few foreigners Danielle genuinely liked. She laughed when he told his heavy Norwegian jokes, and I would occasionally see her reach over and touch him lightly on the arm to get a light for her cigarette. In the old days, in that last summer before she became pregnant, I'd often wondered if they might not have had a little fling on one of those nights when I'd been off to a party in Hóra with Melyá. Anna noticed these slight signs of intimacy, too, and I could feel her gravitating sympathetically to my side of the conversation whenever I had a moment to linger at the table. I thought about the coincidence that she was the same age that Danielle had been when we had met, and like Danielle, was studying law. She had freckles on her nose and cheeks, and her eyes, which stared at you with disturbing frankness, were a startling cornflower blue, as bright and hopeful as spring.

How Mémis was managing to maintain things with Lili and still be able to come back for another day of work seemed like an ongoing miracle to me. He was at the tavérna until late at night, helping us clean up and always at his post in the morning for breakfast. Yet he never seemed to tire.

Nor did Theológos. In sharp contrast to Démetra, Lámbros, Sávas, and myself, all of us as pale gray as unbaked pastry, with increasingly dark circles forming under our bleary, bloodshot eyes, Theológos was looking better than I had seen him in years, as sleek as a well-fed seal. His skin was deeply tanned from the days he was spending ferrying tourists around the island on his caïque, and his brown hair and mustache were sheened with gold by the sun and salt air.

Whenever he could, he would bring a boatload of customers out to Livádi, hoving into sight around the corner of the bay, imperious at the tiller, Panama hat perched on his head, dark dime-store sunglasses fixed on his destination. Sávas and Lámbros would race down the beach to help with the landing as Theológos guided the boat across the bay to a perfect gliding stop at the pier.

The customers that he had corralled in Skála, often twenty at a time, were packed into the interior and clinging to handrails on the decks. They were usually middle-aged and middle-class Greeks off on an intramural spree to their nation's islands. At The Beautiful Helen, Theológos would herd them to their places at tables that we lined up for the occasion, and then, instead of helping the boys and me with the serving, he would sit at the best end, commandeering orders from us as if he were presiding over the captain's table on a transoceanic cruise.

In the evenings he would briefly help with the serving but was soon hanging out with his Patmian cronies in a back corner of the dining area while I did my increasingly exhausted best to make the foreigners happy. And at the end of the night, while I stumbled back to our house on the hill and the boys flung

themselves into instant sleep on their backroom cots, Theológos, still full of energy, would have his way with Démetra. This
was attested to by Magnus, who once swore that late the previous night he had passed by the darkened tavérna on his way
home from a party and had caught them making love beneath
a table in the shadowy recesses of the terrace, seemingly unable
to wait until they had walked the half a mile up the road to
their house.

I, on the other hand, was now sleeping alone. By the end of
July, my forty-two-year-old body was beginning to crumple
under the strain. When I arrived home at night, at three or four
in the morning, lovemaking or simple sex, or even just a cuddle,
was no longer on the menu of possibilities. Nor, on many
nights, were pre-bed ablutions. I would just tear off my
clothes—or sometimes not—and fall like a felled sequoia into
bed beside poor Danielle, who would then spend the few, precious remaining minutes until dawn shaking and beating on
me to try to stop my horrendous snoring. I knew what it was
like, since I had inherited it from my father and remembered
how it had kept me awake on those increasingly regular occasions when he was sent by my stepmother to sleep in an
upstairs room down the hall from mine and set the walls to
vibrating with the noise he made.

So Danielle and I soon agreed that I would switch rooms
with the children and sleep on Sara's cot while she and Matt
moved into their mother's room. Although the thin, glass-
paneled door between the rooms was hardly effective in muf-
fling my sputtering roars and terrifying gagged silences
between explosions, at least she didn't have to put up with the
near corpse I had become, dead-weighted beside her and reeking no doubt of sweat and booze and rancid Greek cuisine.

How she managed to stick it out during this period still fills
me, as I write this, with wonder and gratitude.

Worse than the snoring, however, was the sudden and alarming eruption of varicose veins, as thick as worms, on the inside of my thighs and calves, the skin around them blotched a hideous pinkish purple. These were accompanied by an increasingly excruciating pain in both legs that could only be relieved by my sitting down—as the ever-wise Alíki insisted I do—and putting my legs up on a table as often as possible. "You'll get used to it," said Alíki. "It's part of the price you have to pay in your business." And Démetra and Theológos, instead of being horrified when they saw the extent of my affliction, smiled—and showed me their own. Their legs were both in much worse condition than mine, Démetra's nearly black with the blood that had accumulated under her skin; the veins on Theológos's legs as gnarled as olive trees. They shrugged and said, "Tee na kánoumeh, Thomá?" with their usual fatality, "What are we going to do?" while vital, young Mémis, still as springy as a sapling, stood by and grinned. Only Sávas and Lámbros, among the Greeks, gave me any sympathy, standing with faces as long and sad as those of Sara and Matt as they gathered like mourners at a funeral to watch me prop my tortured limbs on an out-of-the-way tabletop in the shadows of the indoor dining area.

Somewhere deep inside, a tiny voice was telling me that perhaps I wasn't as young as I used to be, and that it might be time to come to terms with this and settle down. Before it was too late. A customer of mine, a young Greek-American woman who appeared one day for lunch and subsequently vanished, voiced similar concerns, as though, sibyl-like, she knew a lot more about me than I did myself. "You know," she said, out of the blue, "you ought to consider teaching. There's an American-owned prep school in northern Greece that you'd be perfect for. It has a theater. And tennis courts. Here's their phone number. Ask to speak to George Draper. He's the vice president. Tell him I sent you." She wrote down her name, paid the bill, and never returned. It was such a strange encounter, the way she had been so definite about what was best for me, that I was tempted to dismiss it out of hand. But in Greece, you learn to ignore these things at your peril. So I kept the piece of paper.

Meanwhile, the success of the tavérna had gathered a momentum of its own. In a way, The Beautiful Helen now belonged more to the customers and their needs than it did to those of us who worked there. We were simply along for the ride, and it felt impossible, at this speed, to jump off. So every morning, no matter how tired you were or how painful it was, you dragged yourself out of bed with seemingly no other choice but to stand up and force your racked body and foggy brain to grapple once again with this monster you had created. It was a Sisyphean task: rolling the boulder of lunch and dinner up the hill only to see it come crashing back down to the bottom at 3 A.M., a hideous, heavy lump of responsibility ready and waiting the following morning to be pushed back up, inch by torturous inch, throughout the rest of the day until, at night. . . .

On the other hand, no matter how exhausted you were, there was always the daily miracle of an adrenaline rush when the lunchtime crowds came pouring in. It not only kept you going but on top of your game, right on through to the end of the evening, ever charming, ever ready to serve.

The tavérna was now also packed in the evenings, with some people hiring caïques to take them out to Livádi or walking the five miles back and forth from the port just for dinner. And once or twice, a yacht anchored in the bay, its passengers lowering a tender to ferry them ashore to slum at this quaint little spot run by, of all people, an American. Meanwhile, we found the same clientele returning meal after meal, bubbling with the gratitude and satisfaction of having found, several of them said, "a home away from home."

Not even the opening of a snack bar at the far end of the beach disturbed us. It had been set up by an enterprising young Patmian named Théo (short for—what else?—Theológos) in the garden of his aunt's home and had become a welcome alternative to the mob scene at The Beautiful Helen. Théo had been abroad and served fancy salads and toasts and mixed drinks with paper umbrellas in them, and also offered beach chairs with umbrellas; he got himself a sizable crowd for lunch—including, we heard, Melyá and her group of friends from Athens and Europe. But who cared? It was July and there was enough to go around for everybody.

Those last crowded days of the month, as we came closer and closer to the metamorphosis of the August 5 *paneyíri* eve, hurtled by. At one point, I remember seeing Stélios and Varvára standing bewildered on the road outside The Beautiful Helen looking on with astonishment at the horde of diners spilling out of the tavérna and across the road to the beach, where we had put tables under the tamarisk trees. It must have been a Sunday lunch, because the two of them were wearing their churchgoing best, Varvára in a freshly ironed white dress, printed with faded pink-and-lavender flowers, and Stélios sporting his one good pair of pleated, gray trousers, cracked brown shoes, and white shirt (but no tie) buttoned at the collar.

I immediately set aside what I had been doing and came over to them. "It will just be a minute," I said, "and there will be a place—"

"No, Thomá," said Stélios. "It's all right. We just came to see."

"You don't want to eat?!" I cried. "But—"

Varvára smiled at me with her soft, clouded blue eyes. "Another time," she said.

"Thomá!" Lámbros was calling me back into the fray. "The check!"

I turned to Stélios and Varvára. "Wait."

I hurried over to do the bill. When I swiveled around to motion to Varvára and Stélios that the table was theirs, they had gone.

Later, at the house, they smiled apologetically. "A lot of people, Thomá."

※

The last day of July was Lili's birthday, and she decided to throw herself a party. Not at The Beautiful Helen, but on a beach near the northeastern tip of the island. It was called Ágrio Yialí, Wild (or Savage) Seaside, both because of its near lack of cultivation and, perhaps, its distance from the civilizing influence of Hóra and the Monastery of St. John. It was a wonderfully isolated spot that did not yet have a road to it and could therefore be reached only by caïque, a twenty-minute trip from Livádi.

The party would begin after the main evening crowd at The Beautiful Helen had dispersed, sometime around midnight. Danielle and I were invited, as were a few friends of Lili's, foreigners and Greeks. But not Theológos nor Démetra and the boys. Lili wanted to get Mémis away from them and have him as much to herself as possible.

Lately, things had not been going well between them. I knew this only by inference, from a few of the Greek phrases that Lili had recently asked me to give her for her notebook. One of them was, "Why are you late?" and another, "I didn't mean what I said."

Mémis was not only a very attractive young man, but an immensely free spirit who saw little reason to curb his appetites. With his blond curls, hairless body, and satyrlike grin, he had a instantly titillating effect on many of our female clientele, who regularly invited him to join them on a stroll down the beach at night, or into the shelter of the fields behind the tavérna or even, once, into a roadside chapel, for what Madame Hortense in *Zorba the Greek* called a little "boom-boom."

So, occasionally, Mémis was a bit later than usual coming home. And this party, on Lili's part, was intended to be either the end of things or a new beginning.

Danielle, of course, didn't want to go. In all of our years on the island, the only parties she had ever attended were those thrown by the Greeks, and usually only those that were held in the daytime, such as Easter. She had no interest whatsoever in socializing or Euro-American chitchat and, like Varvára and Stélios, felt uncomfortable in the presence of too many people.

I didn't want to go either. I was too tired. My legs hurt. I needed rest. It was a pointless waste of time. Et cetera. But then the devil perched himself on my shoulder and said, "You deserve it. And besides, suppose you miss something?" Anna and Lili were similarly persuasive. Particularly Anna. Magnus had taken to going out fishing with his Greek buddies. He disappeared in the early mornings and did not return until late afternoon, laden with his stinking catch for her to clean and cook. So she would spend the days by herself on the beach and at the tavérna, looking a little lost amid the camaraderie of all the summer's old acquaintances. "Does Magnus always go fishing like this?" she asked as I was serving her a salad. "Yes," I replied. "Don't worry, it's not you. It's what Magnus does. A man thing. Hanging out with the boys."

She looked at me with those wide blue eyes. "Then why did he ask me to come to Patmos?"

Beyond her, out on the beach, I could see Danielle walking along the water's edge looking at the surf curling at her feet. In the distance, the children were off playing by themselves.

"He didn't want to be alone," I said and smiled at Anna. It took her a moment, but she laughed.

Danielle also thought I should go to the party. "Let Theoló-gos get up early and do the cooking for a change," she said. This, of course, was not in the cards. First of all, he already did get up early, but it was to head into Skála to shop and afterward to hustle customers for excursions on his caïque. Second, I had no intention of putting my reputation as a cook in his hide-bound, rocklike hands.

But the clincher on my going was provided by Mémis, who at one point said, "Thomá, you are coming, yes? Maybe we'll see the ghosts!"

"What ghosts?"

He looked quickly around. "You don't know? Of the mur-dered Nazi? And . . ." Theológos was entering the kitchen. Mémis immediately dropped his voice to a whisper. "I'll tell you later, when we get there."

Savage Seaside

"Where is the party?" Theológos asked when I said I'd be going.

"Ágrio Yialí," I replied.

"Ágrio Yialí?!" Surprised, Theológos turned to Mémis. "Why there?"

"Ee Lili toh théli," he replied. "Lili wants it."

Theológos looked at him for a moment. "It's far."

"Yes," said Mémis.

"And at night."

Mémis shrugged. "What can we do?!" He hoisted a bucket of potatoes and took them out back to peel.

But Theológos seemed pleased that I had decided to go. He and Démetra both knew that a break in the routine would be good for me and had insisted I leave early, Démetra promising that in the morning she would make the moussaka exactly according to my recipe so I wouldn't have to show up too early. With the changeover of tourists at the end of the month, there were few customers at The Beautiful Helen that night. Nor would there be all that many the following day. Meanwhile, Danielle and the children, as was their habit, had gone back to the house hours before. "You sleep as late as you want tomorrow," she said. "I'll take the children out early." She turned to them. "We'll be very quiet for Papa, yes?"

Sara nodded with great seriousness, her pigtails swinging. "Yes." She grabbed Matt. "Say 'Yes, Tom.'"

Matt grinned. "No!"

※

There was no wind, and a scimitar of the new moon hung overhead as Mémis and I left in the skiff he had wrangled from a friend in the valley. It had a forty-horsepower outboard engine, though, and soon we were skimming across the sea as if it were hardly there, into the path of the moonlight.

I wanted to ask him more about the ghosts then and there but the noise of the engine was horrendous. Besides, he didn't seem in a mood to talk, his gaze intent on the waters in front of us, somber, it seemed, for the first time in his young adult life.

Lili, Magnus, Anna, and the others were already at the beach, and we could soon see the beacons of the fires they had built flickering in the distance.

Out on the sea, as soon as Mémis's boat had slapped water and spray had hit my face, all the exhaustion I had felt at the end of the evening was instantly washed away. There is something about being on the sea that always spells adventure, especially at night, when the darkness surrounding you seems dense with the unknown.

Lili's figure stood out long before we could distinguish any of the others on the beach. She was enveloped in white, gossamer layers of diaphanous cotton that wafted like smoke around her with her every movement, even when there was hardly a breeze to lift them, and as we glided to a stop on the beach, we could see that these clouds were briefly revealing and then tantalizingly misting over the fact that underneath it all, she was wearing absolutely nothing.

"*Fántasma?*" I asked Mémis, joking. "Ghost?"

Mémis shook his head. "No," he answered. "*Mágissa.*"

Sorceress.

He wasn't smiling.

Lili floated down to the shoreline to greet us, arms outstretched, enveloping Mémis in her folds.

Behind her, over the embers of another fire, the charred carcass of a sacrificed goat, its skin a glistening, dripping, reddish brown, was being turned on a spit by Magnus, who squatted at one end as Anna leaned over the center, her breasts tanned and loose inside her pale orange cotton shirt, brushing the beast with a cluster of fresh thyme branches dipped in olive oil and lemon juice.

Jens, Gunnar, and Carl were also there, having arrived together the week before just for Lili's party. As usual, Gunnar and Carl were haggard and unshaven and as pale as fish bellies from weeks of filming and editing, while a fully bronzed Jens, who had been outdoors in Oslo building a boat he intended to one day sail to Greece, was radiant with the first retsina he had had since he'd left. With him was his girlfriend, Lisbet, a dark-haired, warm-bosomed boutique owner from Oslo, who, said Magnus, had been patiently waiting almost ten years for a marriage proposal.

Chrístos, from the travel agency in Skála, sat on a rock near another fire, cradling his guitar, while a lithe young blonde from Australia named Penny lounged at his feet, head on his thigh, gazing at the fire.

Beyond the beach, barely visible in the faint light of the moon, an abandoned farmhouse, its whitewashed plaster exterior cracked and crumbled, sat in the midst of a broad overgrown field that was bounded by shadowy hillsides rising into the darkness.

Mémis, usually counted on to buoy the rest of us up with his bubbling enthusiasms, was definitely not himself. Perhaps because of Lili. He was much too young to know how to deal with a woman of her age and sophistication. And needs. At the beginning of July, everything had seemed possible. Now the cracks and complications were beginning to show.

We ripped into the goat, filled our plates with the various Norwegian salads Lili and Anna had prepared out of potatoes and beans and beets and pasta, and gathered around the fire. For a while, there was nothing but the sounds of chewing and appreciative moans and grunts and sighs. We toasted Lili's birthday several times in the Scandinavian manner, downing shots of the lethal aquavit that Gunnar and Carl had brought for the occasion and chasing it with beer. Then Christos took up his guitar and sang a few plaintive Greek love songs about young girls pining for their husbands and boyfriends taken by a war in the Balkans, and young men cursing unrequited love and the bitterness of the sea.

Finally, I could stand it no longer.

"Mémis," I said, "tell us about the ghosts!"

"Yes!" cried Lili. She turned to the others. "This is why I wanted to have my party here. He told me there are ghosts. He wouldn't tell me what ghosts, though. And he was a little afraid to come"—she turned to him—"weren't you?"

Mémis looked at her, his unkempt blond curls gleaming in the firelight, blue eyes wide with innocence. He gave a manly shrug of indifference.

Christos spoke to him with the same hard look that I had

seen in Theológos's eyes when he'd learned we were going to Ágrio Yialí. *"Fantásmata?"* he asked. "Ghosts?"

"Ksérees," Mémis replied. "You know."

"No," said Chrístos in English. "I don't know."

Everyone looked at Mémis. He hesitated, looked at Chrístos again, then at me.

"Mémis, go on! Please!" implored Lili. She turned to Chrístos. "It's my birthday. I love ghost stories!"

"Thomá," said Mémis, "you translate?"

I nodded.

He sipped his retsina and glanced out at the darkness beyond the fire. His eyes became a little playful then, enjoying the full-fledged attention he was getting, and he leaned forward, looked at each of us in turn, and whispered, *"Énas eétan Yermahnikós aksiomatikós . . ."*

"One was a German officer . . . a Nazi," I translated. "He was called *Capitánios Tromerós,* Captain 'Terrible' or 'Frightening,' because of the horrible things he did to the Patmians. And he had this boyfriend, a young Greek . . ."

"Élla, Mémi!" said Chrístos. "Come on!"

"It's true!" said Mémis.

Chrístos answered him in Greek. "How do you know? You weren't even born!"

"Everybody says so!" replied Mémis, also in Greek.

"Who?"

"There are lots of people—*Livadióti*—who remember!"

Lili grabbed my arm. "What're they saying?"

Chrístos stood up. "Many stories!" he said in English to all of us. "You know how people are. They make everything worse and everything better than it really is. Nothing is the truth. Not even in the history books! Right, Thomá?" He helped Penny to her feet. "We have to go. I have lots of customers coming in the morning." He looked around. "Anybody else want a ride?"

There were, of course, no takers.

Lili turned to us after Chrístos and Penny had departed for Skála in his tiny, cabined caïque. "What's the matter with him?" she asked.

Mémis shrugged. I knew, though, what was bothering Chrístos. Mémis was telling one of many stories that were not meant for the ears of foreigners. They were Patmian stories. About family. And even I had not heard this one.

"So?" said Anna, leaning eagerly toward Mémis and smiling at me. "Go on."

"Yes!" the others chimed in, Magnus, Jens, Lizbet, Gunnar, and Carl drawing even closer to the fire. The juices from the roasted goat glistened on their lips and fingers.

Mémis's chest swelled, his eyes shining, and he continued. "*Étsi . . .*"

"This young boyfriend. Was he a Patmian?" asked Magnus.

Mémis hesitated. "I—don't know," he said. And then continued, "*Alá—*"

"But—" I went on, "he was a Nazi informer, and the Greek resistance ordered both of them abducted and taken to Arkoi—" I pointed across the sea. "A little island over there— to be picked up by a British submarine."

Mémis leaned forward.

"So a group of Patmian men," he whispered, "sent another boy, fourteen, fifteen years old, that Capitánios Tromerós was also interested in—and maybe even had forced to have sex with him already, I don't know—to make a rendezvous to meet the captain and his friend at a beach outside of Skála. When they got there, the Patmians were waiting. They grabbed them, tied them up, and put them both in a rowboat and brought them here. To wait for a caïque to take them to Arkoi. It was in the summer, on a night like this, in July . . ."

He looked around him, into the darkness beyond the civilizing light of the slowly dying fire.

"And?" asked Carl, voice cracking.

Mémis continued. "The boyfriend kept saying how he was innocent, how he hated the captain, how the captain had made him do it. But of course, they all knew what an informer he was. Meanwhile, the other boy was staring at them, his eyes full of hatred, burning like coals. They took the captain and his friend to that house—" Mémis pointed into the shadows beyond the beach where the old abandoned farmhouse was barely visible, gray and ghostly in the darkness. "To wait for the caïque. But then, one of the Patmians couldn't wait. Or maybe it was all of them. There was so much hatred. And one of them grabbed a gun and, before anyone could stop him, shot the Nazi. After that, of course—"

Mémis paused and looked around at our mesmerized faces.

"—they had to shoot his boyfriend, the Greek informer, too."

He pointed toward the field behind us.

"The bodies are buried out there somewhere. The Greek resistance was very angry. So were the Germans. They never found the bodies. So there was revenge. The Germans shot some Patmians. And the men who had abducted Capitánios Tromerós, who had wanted to be heroes, couldn't even tell anyone about what they'd done. But everyone knew . . ."

There was a brief silence as Mémis stared into the fire. The wind had completely dropped and there was not a sound from anywhere. Even the crickets seemed to have paused.

"The Patmióti say the ghosts walk here in Ágrio Yialí," Mémis continued, "waiting for someone to find their bodies. That they walk on summer nights like this." He looked around and dropped his voice to a deep whisper. "Especially on July 31 . . ."

Lili shrieked. And hugged him. "Isn't he wonderful?!" she cried. We all laughed.

"Come!" said Lili, rising and pulling Mémis up with her.

She started dragging him toward the rocks at the end of the headland.

"Mémi—wait!" cried Magnus.

Lili laughed. "It's my birthday!" she yelled as they disappeared into the darkness.

Magnus looked at the rest of us. Then he asked the question that was on all our minds. "Do you suppose they're all still alive? Here on Patmos? Those men? The other boy?"

"They could be," I said.

"My God!" said Carl.

We sat there for a while staring at the fire, contemplating a Patmos we had never before imagined, so far away from the postcards and legends, the tales of miracle-working icons, man-eating monsters, and even petrified Yénoupas in the harbor.

A sudden howl caused the hairs to rise on the back of my neck. We swiveled around. Mémis, completely naked, emerged from behind the rocks at the end of the beach carrying an equally naked, screaming, thrashing Lili toward the water, where they both splashed, stumbled, and fell, convulsed with laughter, into the sea.

A drunken Gunnar staggered to his feet. "Have to go," he mumbled. Carl quickly agreed. As did Jens and Lizbet.

The party was over.

※

On the ride back to Livádi, Lili was all smiles. Mémis, sodden with aquavit and wine, was smiling too, but there was a manic quality to the way he slammed the throttle wide open and cut across the swells at an angle guaranteed to produce the roughest and wettest ride possible.

On the beach I found out why. As Mémis was out in the shallows securing the boat, Lili gathered Magnus, Anna, and myself around her—Jens and the others having roared back to Skála in his massive inflatable outboard.

"He's coming with me, to Oslo!" she whispered. "I'm going to find him work on a film!"

While Anna was embracing her, Magnus and I looked at each other with the skepticism of old Greek hands who had heard similar statements from smitten foreigners more times than we cared to remember.

All of us then went down to the water's edge to help Mémis carry the debris from the party up to the shadows of the darkened, silent tavérna, where we stored them under a table.

As we were trudging through the sand, Magnus said, "Mémi, it was the boy, wasn't it?"

Mémis kept on walking. "What boy?"

"Who shot the German officer."

Mémis shrugged.

"Who was he?" Magnus continued. "He must still be here on the island. And the others, too, yes?"

Mémis stopped. "Who knows? I hear only the story. No names. Never names. You know." He looked at me. "Nobody wants names."

Magnus didn't believe him, but gave up asking. They all wished me good night, and the four of them started off on the road up to Lili's house.

As I turned inland to take the path to my house, Mémis came racing back toward the tavérna.

"We forgot the aquavit!" he yelled.

He motioned to me to wait for him, and after he had rescued the bottle from the pile of things under the table, he took me aside, away from whomever might be awake and listening inside The Beautiful Helen.

"Thomá," he whispered, his eyes wide and shining in the light from the roadside lamp, blond hair glowing, "You know, they say the other boy was Theológos! That *he* shot the captain!"

Before I could reply, he ran off into the night, waving the bottle of aquavit.

Apocálypsi

Suddenly, the eve of the *paneyíri* was upon us, bearing down like a tidal wave, and for the next four days there was no time to think of anything else.

Theológos and the owners of the cafés in Upper Livádi spent their mornings in Skála scrambling among the smallest vegetable sellers and farmers for whatever scraps were left of the island's meager supplies of potatoes, onions, tomatoes, and cucumbers. Meanwhile, at the butcher's, every available goat and chicken, spoken and paid for weeks in advance, were slaughtered, thrown into a truck, and carried out to the valley. Theológos had also had a couple of goats tethered in his plot of land behind the tavérna and these he dispatched the day before the feast, right out on the beach as our customers were having lunch, and then trundled their stripped remains up to us in a wheelbarrow, his hands, arms, and pants legs drenched in blood.

✳

Over the years, I had regularly attended the celebrations at the village and the beach and knew that compared to The Beautiful Helen, the two cafés in Upper Livádi were small potatoes. Both operated out of what were little more than single-room stone huts on the edge of the tiny cobbled square outside the village church. Each had room enough for a maximum of four tiny tables indoors and six to ten outside in the square. By mutual agreement, they hung colored lightbulbs across the square and set up a rudimentary speaker system to pipe out recorded music from the café belonging to Stélios and Varvára's son-in-law, Alékos. While the cafés would be packed with celebrants from eight until midnight, this would amount to hardly half the number of people attending the festivities at the beach, and when the cafés closed, most of their clientele, plus their owners, would descend for more of the same at The Beautiful Helen, where there would be live music and no time limit to the evening.

After at least fifteen years of doing this, Theológos had developed a system, and I gladly staggered aside to become a cog in his jerry-built but reasonably well-functioning machine. For the evening, at least, The Beautiful Helen was once again all his.

The orchestra—electrified bouzouki, lute, *baglamá* (a tiny bouzouki), and a Greek type of zither called the *sandoóri*—had been hired through a cousin on the nearby island of Kalymnos. Theológos had gotten them for next to nothing with promises of tips from the many party goers who would pay to have their favorite songs and dances played over and over again, occasionally showering the musicians and dancing area with drachma notes to further show their appreciation.

For efficiency's sake, the evening's menu would include only two main dishes—goat stewed in red wine with onions and tomatoes and a heaping plate of the fried, finger-sized *maridáki*, whitebait, which were then plentifully in season and supplied by our regular fishermen customers. There would be French-fried potatoes (of which there would never be enough), a tomato, cucumber, and onion salad (feta could no longer be found on the island), bread, and, of course, the enormous reserve of beer, wine, and soft drinks that Theológos had stock-piled over the past six weeks. The beverages, with their profit margin of 80 percent, were our gold mine.

During the morning and afternoon, while Démetra was cooking and poor Mémis was hard at work peeling and slicing a mountain of potatoes and dropping them into water-filled buckets, Theológos and the boys carried long planks down to the beach and set them up on large plastic olive barrels and cinder blocks to serve as tables and benches, enough to cover the beach from the road to the water and to seat perhaps two to three times as many people as the cafés in Upper Livádi. While they were doing this, I stayed at my post to cook and serve what I could muster of our usual luncheon fare.

Where were Danielle, Sara, and Matt during all of this? I hardly remember. They had become so marginal to the pressures I was facing that they seemed to have faded from existence, like figures in a photograph left out too long in the sun, smiling and squinting at the camera, somewhat puzzled-looking, caught in a barely recalled summer moment. But there would be time for them later. After I had raked in my profits.

At 4 P.M. we stopped serving customers and began making the final arrangements for the evening. We cleared out the inner dining area and rearranged the glass-fronted display cases and the kitchen tables into a kind of buffet counter at which our clientele would line up, choose what they wanted to eat, and carry it out to the tables themselves.

"Démetra will stay in the kitchen with Mémis to cook and make the salads," ordered Theológos. "Sávas and Lámbros will serve the food, and Thomá, you will give them what they want to drink. I will be at the end of the line"—he pointed at a small table near the door, on top of which was the cigar box that would serve as his cash register—"to do their bills and take the money." He smiled at me. *"Kouráyio, Thomá!"* he said. "Courage! Tonight is the night!" And he slapped me on the back.

At 7 P.M., the musicians set themselves up on a small platform in a corner of the dining area just outside the serving area and hurried in to get something to eat before the festivities started.

A half hour later, the first customers—families with children, including mine, I believe—began to show up. By eight-thirty, it was dark outside, and what soon became an endless parade of diners started filing past the counters.

In the beginning, everything proceeded in a cheerful, civilized manner, the customers' requests quickly processed, their plates heaped with food and well worth the exorbitant fee Theológos was charging, with places available for everyone at the tables outside.

Then, as the orchestra started tuning up and began playing, the tenor of the evening quickly began to change. As with most Greek sources of music, the higher the noise level, the better. It is for this reason that the Greeks are second to none, not even Americans, in their fondness for monstrous, megawatt jukeboxes turned up to their highest possible level even in the smallest cafés. So you can imagine what it's like when live musicians, who needed absolutely no amplification at all, were nevertheless given the entire outdoors, including the eastern Aegean, at which to blast away. You can also imagine what it must have been like to be standing there serving dinner inside an essentially closed space right next to the bandstand and speakers.

While the musicians were playing—which, as they began to rake in the tips, was almost nonstop—it became impossible to communicate without ripping apart your vocal cords to try and top the nerve-jangling, banjo-like ripple and pound of the electrified bouzouki and *baglamá*. The customers would shout at us, and we would shout at them, and soon, shouting at one another became tinged with a certain hysteria and anger, even when this was not what you intended.

On top of that, the longer I stood there, the more the pain in my legs increased. But stand I had to, because the top of the refrigerated display case from which I was handing out drinks was shoulder-high, so I couldn't sit down behind it without disappearing from view.

I tried to remember that poor Démetra had this same condition and would glance back at her for inspiration and sympathy. She stood at the stove, her face dripping with perspiration, lit up by leaping gas fires as she shifted from one huge skillet to another, shaking batches of sizzling potatoes and whitebait, as resilient as ever. I would briefly feel ashamed at my own frailty, but then I would look over Theológos, also phlebetic, and see him seated comfortably at his cashier's table contentedly stuffing money in the cigar box or emptying it into a shoe box on a chair behind him—and my agony, fired by resentment and self-pity, would once again mount toward the unbearable.

Miraculously—and with the aid of more than a little retsina—I withstood the worst of it and remained upright and functioning even as my impressions of the evening descended into a sloshing phantasmagoria of sounds and sights.

At one point (I have no idea what time it was) I remember Danielle and the children coming up to say good night. I don't recall Lili being there, nor Magnus, Anna, or the other Norwegians. Only waves of shouting, smiling, pleading faces lit from below by the light in the refrigerator's glass front, while behind their heads, a string of colored bulbs, which Theológos had hung along the inside tavérna wall, haloed their hair in blue, red, and green.

Beyond the tavérna's front door was the party, but I could barely glimpse it, this wonderful, raucous evening that had been the highlight of every summer in Livádi and so special a part of Danielle's and my past. I might as well have been on a mountaintop in another part of the island. Rumors would reach us of the bacchanalia in progress—people dancing upon the tabletops, someone fainting, another cut by a broken bottle—but they scarcely penetrated the noise of the music and the shell that I had thrown up to shelter myself from the confusion and the continuing pain in my legs.

At one point, however, the fog lifts and I remember Alékos appearing. I was astonished, because this meant it must be after midnight, since he wouldn't have come down if he had not closed his café in the square. Pétros, the owner of the other café, was with him, both looking very jolly and slightly drunk. "Eh, Thomá!" shouted Alékos. "Beautiful, huh?! Many people!"

"Yes?!" I said. I glanced at Theológos, busy at his table by the door making change out of the cigar box, and then turned back to our two competitors. "How much did you take in?"

"A lot!" said Pétros.

"Sixty-five thousand!" said Alékos.

"For me," said Pétros, "sixty!"

"*Beéra, Thomá!*" shouted Alékos. "Beer! Give us beer!"

Sometime later, about 4 A.M., everything suddenly ceased. The music stopped, the musicians quickly packed up and disappeared, and all but a few sodden customers abruptly vanished. I stepped cautiously out from behind my refrigerator. The floor was littered with various bits of paper and food and slippery with spilled drinks.

While Theológos began counting the take, I staggered outside for a breath of fresh air and a table where I could prop up my feet.

The devastation was appalling. Goat bones and other garbage were strewn across the tabletops and the sand. Empty bottles and glasses, whole and broken, many with the remains of cigarettes disintegrating inside, dotted the landscape, glittering like giant hailstones in the glare spilling from the tavérna. Fortunately, it was still dark outside. Shortly afterward, in the pitiless gray light of dawn, it would become truly depressing, a plowed-up graveyard of the evening's appetites, left for us to somehow set right.

But first we had to eat—and to see how much money we had made. Démetra called me inside, where she and the boys had quickly set up a table. It was heaped, not with leftovers, but with a feast of the very best portions of the goat stew, which she had put aside early in the evening. There were freshly fried potatoes and *marídes* still sizzling from the pan, and even chunks of supposedly unobtainable feta in the salad.

Theológos came to sit at the head of the table, the paper on which he had been doing his calculating in hand. We all looked at him expectantly. He beamed in return.

"How much?" I said.

"Very good!" he answered.

"How much?"

He paused dramatically. "Forty thousand drachmas!" He smiled with great satisfaction and began spooning goat onto his plate.

For a moment, I couldn't speak. Then I said, "That can't be right."

He looked at me with wide-eyed innocence, taking some potatoes.

"Why not?"

"Because," I replied, my voice rising but still under control, "Alékos and Pétros told me they made sixty-five thousand apiece!"

He stared at me for a moment, and then smiled. "Thomá," he said, "you think they are telling the truth?"

"Why not?"

"Because they want to look like—how do you say?—big shots." He gingerly picked up a hot whitebait and bit off its head. "Come on, let's eat, and then I will count again. You can watch me."

Nausea was stirring in my stomach.

"Let's do the counting now."

There was complete silence in the room.

"Okay," he said, pushing back his chair.

He went over to the table and opened the cigar and shoe

boxes. Both were stuffed with banknotes—one-hundred-, five hundred-, and thousand-drachma denominations. There were also piles of coins.

Nobody said a word. Démetra, the boys, and Mémis occupied themselves with their food. I sat in my place at the table. I should have gone and stood over Theológos to see every note that he was counting, but I couldn't bring myself to do this. Absurdly, I still wanted to maintain some semblance of trusting him.

When he finished, he looked up at me.

"Thomá," he said. "You were right. It's more."

My heart leapt. There was still a chance that honesty would prevail.

"How much?" I asked.

He looked me straight in the eye and said, "Forty-nine thousand."

I was speechless. His brazen ability to lie like that in front of his sons and Démetra and Mémis, and to lie to me, a man who had been his friend for nine years and was perhaps the only person on the island who trusted him, took my breath away, literally.

Finally, I managed to mumble, "Well, that's better!" Or something. And everybody smiled with relief and resumed eating. Meanwhile, I sat there unable to touch my food, immobilized by this sudden revelation of how blindly trusting I had been, how laughably naïve. And all my grand and shattered illusions began to sink in a swamp of humiliation.

There is a saying in Greece that comes down from Byzantine times, one recently recounted to me by a New York Greek to whom I told this story. In business, the Byzantines said, you are responsible only for your own success, and if you have a partner, it is up to him to look after himself. So the saying, still applicable today, is, "Better to be thought a thief than a fool."

Well, that night at The Beautiful Helen, there was absolutely no question about who was who.

Just Desserts

Transfigurations

Danielle, of course, could have said "I told you so," but—much to my surprise, not to mention shame—she reached out to console me.

It was the next morning, the actual feast of the Transfiguration, and we were sitting on the bed talking. I don't remember if I had gone straight home and awakened Danielle or if I slept first. I think I slept—what little I could—and then we talked.

"I'm going to quit," I said.

"Good!" she said.

Immediately, I began to reconsider. "Yeah, but—"

"Look at your legs!" she said.

I glanced down at them, something which I'd lately been learning not to do. From the stress of the evening, one of the veins now had a nasty new bulge in it, larger than any of those on even Theológos's calves.

"Let's go back to Rethymnon," Danielle continued. "Home."

And Sara, sitting at the end of the bed, cried out, "Home?! We can go home?!" with Matt, from the corner, immediately chiming in: "On the boat! The boat!"

✻

I took the first really hot bath that I had had in weeks, washed my hair, put on clean clothes, and headed down to the tavérna with Danielle and the children.

On the way, we saw Stélios in his field. He cheerfully waved. *"Oráyo vrádi!"* he shouted. "Beautiful evening!"

"Were you there?!" I called out.

He laughed. "Don't you remember?"

"Óy-hee!" No.

Theológos was sitting on an upturned beer crate just inside the dining area, undershirt on, pants legs rolled up to his calves, flip-flops on his feet, fashioning the end piece of a hawser, entwining it back upon itself and wrapping it with tape.

All the detritus of the *paneyíri* had disappeared, and the tavérna and beach looked as they had on any other morning, clean and fresh for another day in paradise.

Démetra, already cooking in the kitchen, saw me as I approached.

"Kaliméra, Thomá! Kimeéthikess kalá?" she called out. "Good morning! Did you sleep well?"

I waved back without saying anything.

Theológos squinted up at me in the morning sun. *"Yásoo, Thomá!* How are you?"

"Not good," I said.

At that moment, just as they say happens to a drowning man, all of those years at The Beautiful Helen came back to me, flashing by in a single instant. I saw the golden days of that first summer when Eléni (had she ever really existed?) was still with us and the boys were innocent little children. The mornings and afternoons were soft with sunlight dappled by the ancient tamarisk tree rising from the terrace. I remembered bringing Sara down to the tavérna for her first experience of the sand and sea, and the blustery winter afternoons when storms from the south sent the normally placid waters of the bay crashing in giant, roiling waves upon the shore as we sat inside The Beautiful Helen, steaming up its windows with talk and laughter and great quantities of ouzo.

There were those epic spring evenings before the tourist season began when someone's name day or wedding or baptism or just the holy action of *kéfi* itself would suddenly bring people together in The Beautiful Helen, and there would be a party, and much dancing, the women in their dainty circles, the men turning themselves in great acrobatic leaps on the fulcrum of a partner's handkerchief. And that memorable morning the first September when Danielle had left me alone at home to return to her own house to paint, and I had subsequently staggered down to the tavérna, my heart suddenly beating so hard that I thought it would break my ribs, gasping for a doctor, and Theológos had smiled and offered me a cognac instead, saying, "You'll be all right, Thomá. You're just in love."

"Teé éhees?" Theológos asked, squinting up at me.

"Thomá," Démetra called out, still within the kitchen, "how many eggs do you put in the béchamel, for the moussaka?"

"Just a second," I answered. And turned back to Theológos.

I could feel the rage, the humiliation of it all threatening to swallow me in a paroxysm of sputtering. I tried to remain calm, to concentrate on what Danielle and I had decided I was going to say. I would demand my money back or threaten to tell everyone on the island what he had done. And I would also quit. On the spot.

"Thomá!" cried Mémis, appearing from the storage area. "No more potatoes! What're we going to do?"

I ignored him.

"Theológo," I said, "I want my money back."

"What—?"

"Every week you've been telling me to wait for the *paneyíri.* Week after week, no profits! Just wait! And then last night you tell me that we made only forty-nine thousand!" My voice began to rise out of control. "Even when Pétros and Alékos made sixty, sixty-five thousand apiece! You said they were the liars. How stupid do you think I am," I screamed, *"maláka?!"*

This was a terrible insult: the worst thing you can say to a Greek male is to call him a masturbator. While you hear Greeks using this epithet jokingly among themselves, it would be a horrible mistake for a foreigner to do so. But I wasn't joking. Theológos dropped the rope and stood up, face flushing purple and red. He grabbed me by the throat. And just as quickly, Mémis, Danielle, and then Démetra rushed over to pull him off. Sara and Matt started crying, terrified. Danielle knelt to take them in her arms.

"What do you want, Theológo?" I shouted. "To kill me?! Like you did that Nazi?!"

The blood drained from Theológos's face as he stopped struggling against Mémis's and Démetra's grip.

Out on the road, a group of straw-hatted foreign tourists with beach blankets and inflated children's toys paused to stare with uncomprehending curiosity at the tirade I continued to launch at Theológos, all in Greek.

"I quit!" I screamed. "And I want all my money back, the entire hundred and fifty thousand—and if you don't give it to me—tomorrow"—I was now thoroughly in orbit, not thinking at all as I shouted—"I'm going to the police!"

There was a sudden, profound silence.

The tourists whispered among themselves and moved on, glancing over their shoulders as they walked away.

Theológos looked at Mémis and then at me.

"Who told you that?" he said. "About the Nazi?"

"It's no secret," I quickly replied.

"That I was there?"

I hesitated. "Maybe."

Theológos glanced at Danielle and the children.

"You talk, but you don't know anything, Thomá!" I could see

the anger coming back, his face reddening. "That man was a monster! What he did to us! He deserved—"

Suddenly Sávas and Lámbros came running around the outside corner of the tavérna shouting, "We found tomatoes!"

I stared at them, these teenagers who to me were still little boys, almost my own sons.

Theológos turned to them. "Good," he said.

The redness in his face faded, and he took a deep breath and reached down to pick up the hawser he had been working on, smoothing out the tape on its end. Then, in a low voice, he said to me, "Okay. I'll give it back to you."

I couldn't answer.

"Fifty thousand now," he continued, "and the rest tomorrow." He paused. "All right?"

As the anger evaporated from my body, I was suddenly cold, and so weak I thought my legs might collapse under me.

"Okay," I replied.

"Listen," Theológos continued, clearing his throat. "I can't work in the tavérna today. I have a big group of tourists to take over to the island of Leros. I won't be back until late tonight. They're expecting me in Skála in half an hour. If you could stay to help? Just today?"

"Thomá?" Démetra said, eyes pleading.

"Please?" asked Theológos.

I didn't dare look at Danielle, not being able to believe what I was about to do. But I took a deep breath and did it anyway.

"Okay," I said. "Okay. But only today."

Démetra's gold tooth flashed with her smile. Mémis's face remained impassive. The boys stood there trying to understand what had happened, confused grins on their faces.

"Thank you," said Theológos.

I looked over at him.

And said nothing.

End Time

"You are crazy," Danielle declared as soon as we were alone.

"I can't just walk out on them like that," I answered. "Déme-tra and the boys and Mémis. They need help. And time to find someone else."

"That's their problem! You don't owe them anything!"

"They aren't Theológos," I said.

✳

In the late afternoon, as we were preparing dinner, a huge black yacht, a three-masted schooner, really, appeared around the corner of the bay, dark sails furled, and glided majestically to a stop in its center, anchoring about three hundred yards off the beach.

We stared at it for a long, long time, waiting for someone to appear on deck and lower a boat to come ashore, but no one did, not anyone we could see. It seemed eerily uninhabited, as silent and mysterious about its intentions as that black mono-lith in the movie *2001*.

After a while, we forgot about the ship and went back to cooking, and as night fell, its presence completely went out of our minds, disappearing into the darkness.

It was a Saturday, and the tavérna was once again packed. Nevertheless, I found a moment—actually, took one—to step aside from the madness to have a quick cigarette, sneaking off into the shadows just beyond the light that fell on the dining area.

As I was standing there, feeling immensely relieved to be soon out of this job and its crushing disappointment, a young woman emerged from the darkness of the beach and came up to me. She was about twenty, beautiful, darkly tanned, with long, straight black hair, sparkling brown eyes, and a beauty mark per-fectly placed at the corner of her mouth. Following behind her

was a handsome middle-aged man, dressed in white, hair graying at his temples, whom I imagined to be her lover.

"Hi!" she said with a soft French accent. "Remember me?"

"Sure," I replied, lying.

"Good!" she said and smiled. "I've never forgotten your
tavérna." She paused and then cheerfully continued, "I was wondering. I want to bring some friends for dinner tomorrow. Could
you make us those same two specialties, you know, the Chinese
Chicken with Cucumbers and that curry?"

Suddenly I did remember her—that beauty mark at the corner of her mouth—and the group that she had been with, fifteen
friends from France, at the very beginning of the summer.

She glanced at her companion. "It was so delicious!" she said
and then turned back to me. "Okay? Eight people? Tomorrow
night?"

Her brown eyes were luminous in the faint light from the
tavérna, full of expectation, and I hated what I had to say.

"I'm sorry. This is my last night."

"What do you mean?"

"I'm not working here any longer after tonight."

"Why?!"

"I—have a problem with the owner. My partner. I'm leaving."

"But can't you stay for one more night?" She looked suddenly much younger, a little girl, crushed.

"It's impossible. I'm sorry."

The man stepped forward.

"Excuse me," he said. "I don't mean to interrupt, but this
young lady is my daughter. Tomorrow is her birthday. Last
night, I told her she could have a party anywhere she wanted.
She said here. So we specially sailed over for the occasion.
From Mykonos. That's mine out there."

He pointed at the black schooner, its masts barely visible
among the stars.

"So," he continued, "if you could please reconsider . . ."

At that moment, Danielle and the children arrived for dinner. I could see them standing in the road on the other side of the dining area looking for me. I could also see what else was coming. I had stayed this night for Démetra and the boys. Tomorrow it would be for this young woman. And the next day, something else would come up. My legs were killing me. My family was waiting.

Since that night, I have told many people this story, and they all have wanted me to say that I stayed, just that one extra night, for the young woman's birthday. But Danielle, when I told her moments later about the young woman's request, had cried out, "You didn't say 'yes'!"

No, I didn't. I couldn't. I had learned too much. My capacity for illusions, for deluding myself, had come to an end.

I told the young woman and her father the whole story, how Theológos had been stealing from me all summer, how he had taken the profits that first night when I had asked to make dinner for my departing friends, and how he would take the profits if I stayed to cook for her birthday party.

"I can't do it anymore," I said. "I'm very sorry."

The girl started to plead one more time, but her father touched her arm. "I understand," he said, reaching out to shake my hand. The girl smiled, sad and lovely, and then turned away with her father, the two of them disappearing into the shadows of the tamarisk trees.

Last Things

We went to Skála the next night, Danielle and the children and I, to buy tickets for our journey back to Rethymnon and to have dinner together for the first time since my servitude at The Beautiful Helen had begun.

That afternoon, we had told Stélios and Varvára what had happened with Theológos. They nodded. *"Kséroumeh, Thomá,"* Stélios said. "We knew. But what could we do? You had to find out for yourself!"

Saying good-bye to the boys and Démetra and Mémis had been very hard. But the fact that Theológos was around and that there were customers needing to be served made the farewells blessedly brief. I told Sávas and Lámbros that I would be back soon to see them.

"Seégoura!" they said. "For sure!"

I took the rest of the one hundred and fifty thousand from Theológos and fought back the impulse to reach out and shake his hand. But the thought of the absurdity of it, and of touching again that rough stone paw, held me back.

We looked at each other for a moment, his sharp brown eyes questioning mine, and then I turned and walked away, pocketing the money.

※

In Skála, I told friends how amazed I was that Theológos had acquiesced so quickly about the money.

Chrístos laughed. We were sitting in a café having drinks before dinner, Chrístos, myself, Danielle and the children, Lili, Magnus, Anna, Jens, and Nikos, a retired Greek-American in his sixties who had just returned to Patmos after spending the summer in the States visiting friends. He had listened to my story with considerable amusement, lighting up a cigar afterward but not saying anything.

"Of course he gave it back to you!" said Chrístos. "He was afraid of the police."

"But what could they have done?" I said. "I didn't have a work permit! I was totally illegal."

"But the police had let you work. Hadn't they? So, it's obvious you have some inside connection." Chrístos smiled. "Perhaps the CIA?"

"No!"

He gave me a knowing look. "It doesn't matter. Whatever, it scared Theológos."

"Don't worry about Theológos," said Lili. "He's still keeping all the money he was skimming off the top buying supplies."

Chrístos looked at me. "You didn't ask for that, too?"

I could feel humiliation once again knotting my stomach. "No," I said. "I could never prove how much it was. Besides, I just wanted out."

There was a silence while the waiter set out our drinks.

Then Magnus said to me, "So he murdered the Nazi!"

"Probably."

"What the hell you talking about?!" said Nikos in his brusque American twang, cigar chomped in his mouth.

We had been friends for years, since we had first met out at Livádi and made the incredible discovery that he had known my father back in the States.

Nikos had been born on Patmos around 1930, but had left when he was a teenager, along with a lot of other young Patmian men, including Theológos, to make his fortune abroad. After four decades in America, he had returned home to retire on the considerable sum he had accumulated in the restaurant business, mostly as a waiter. He was such a prosperous American type, always with that big cigar, his full head of silver-white hair carefully coiffed in 1950s wavelets from front to back, that we hadn't been able to resist calling him "Nick the Greek."

When he had mentioned an expensive restaurant he used to work in outside Washington, D.C.—one that my high-rolling father had frequented with clients and lady friends—I had asked if he had known a George Stone. And he had said, "My God! Mr. Stone! Yeah, I knew him! Your father? Jesus! I was his waiter!"

This had made us instant buddies and had been another sign for me that my journeying to Patmos had been more than just a happy accident. Over the years, I had relied on Nikos's advice for many decisions and was now sorry I hadn't tried to reach him when I was heading into this arrangement with Theológos. But of course, he would have given me the same warnings as everyone else, and I would have ignored them, the same as I had the rest.

"Nobody knows who shot that Nazi except the people who were there," he continued. "And they never talked. There were all kinds of stories about what happened and who was involved." He paused. "Most of them ugly. People got killed because of it."

Nikos looked around the table.

"You guys can't imagine what it was like then. Something I won't ever forget. There was no food. The Germans had totally cut us off from the rest of the world. People were scrounging the hills, eating nettles. They were dropping dead in the streets from starvation. I remember—my aunt Zöe . . ." He shook his head. "And then that son-of-a-bitch Nazi captain—*O Tromerós* they called him, 'the terrifying one'—would go strutting around the harbor, and if you looked at him the wrong way— whatever *he* thought was the wrong way—he'd pull out his pistol and fucking shoot you."

He turned to Danielle. "Sorry about the language." He indicated the children.

"It's okay," she said.

Nikos looked at me.

"You ever been out to where Theológos is from? Out there in Ághios Nikólas?"

I nodded, remembering the one time I had visited, when I was researching a book about the island, how struck I had been by the desolation, the north wind coming right at you off the sea, nearly blowing you backward. I had asked an old farmer about the little church that was there, whitewashed stones that seemed to be growing right up from the rocky ground. The farmer had said, "Oh, it is very old!" I asked how old. "Very, very old! Ancient!" he had said, making whirlpools in the air with his hand. *"Pro Xristoú!"* he added. "Before Christ!"

Nick turned to the Norwegians. "Talk about being cut off! Patmos was cut off, Greece was cut off, but Ághios Nikólas! Even today you're lucky you can keep one tomato plant growing on that ground. And what does grow is all bent over, gnarled up, twisted out of shape from the wind and no water. Terrible!"

He relit his cigar.

"So, people were pretty bad off. Even after the war. Which was why I left. Poor?! You don't know what poor is. It eats a hole in you. That never goes away. So you gotta think about that when you start calling them thieves." He glanced at me. "And murderers."

"But Theológos could've been there," Magnus said. "When the Nazi was killed."

Nick looked at him.

"Yeah. I coulda been there too."

We stared at Nikos.

He smiled, his eyes slightly hooded.

"But I wasn't."

He turned back to me. "Your father was just like you, you know? Never counted his change. That's a lot of temptation, Thomá!" He looked at the others. "Big tipper, though, Mr. Stone! Real big tipper!"

※

With the new pier now completed, Skála had become overrun with tourists. It looked like Times Square on Saturday night. And while we were having drinks, a huge cruise ship floated into the harbor, festooned with thousands of lights strung from bow to stern and back again, towering over us like one of those huge electric billboards on Broadway. The closer it got, the smaller we felt.

I thought about Hóra, how desolate it had looked to me the first day I arrived, crumbled and abandoned. Later, I had seen a copy of a sketch scratched on the wall of a monastery chapel, apparently rendered while a seventeenth-century raid on the island was in progress. It shows a formidable Venetian armada (commanded by Francesco Morosini, the same admiral who would later shell the Parthenon) attacking the defenseless Patmian merchant ships in the harbor, overwhelming them.

A Patmian folk song about the same raid describes the devastation that was wrought: "Seven thousand landed," it laments, "to stay for only three hours . . . but the lawless dogs remained for three days! Our oil became rivers, the wheat was scattered everywhere . . . And liquor and wine were spilled on the streets . . ."

Now, however, the Patmians were ready. Buses, taxis, caïques, and motor launches were lined up at the waterfront to ferry tourists anywhere they wanted to go, and new restaurants, coffee and sweet shops, snack bars, and jewelry boutiques were springing up everywhere, with hotels and rooming houses not far behind. There were motorbikes of every size and decibel level to rent. And cars. And boats. And villas. So when summer visitors eventually plodded their laden, satiated way onto a departing ship, they were now the ones who had been nicely plundered. At least, that's the way it seemed.

It was almost impossible for Danielle and the children and me to find a table for dinner, even at the most out-of-the-way little tavérnas hidden in Skála's warren of back streets. When we finally did get a place—in a big restaurant near the port—the service was interminable and the food greasy and lukewarm. Nevertheless, what a joy it was not only to just sit back and be waited on but to eat food cooked by someone else, no matter how bad! And, yes, I left a big tip—not to impress, but to show my heartfelt sympathy.

Finding a taxi to take us back to Livádi was out of the question, particularly because of the imminent arrival of a passenger ferry from the mainland, which would dock as soon as the cruise ship departed. Lili and Magnus and Anna were staying in town to await friends, so Danielle and I tried to get a caïque to take us back right away. Fortunately, one of the Livádi fishermen, Poditós, was in town and shortly ready to return. We arranged to go with him.

As we were waiting on the edge of the fisherman's dock, Lili ran up to us, her notebook in hand. "Tom! One thing!" she cried, coming to a halt and pausing to catch her breath.

"You see, what's happened is—Mémis and I had a long talk last night. I don't think he's ready to come to Oslo. Matter of fact, I know he's not. It's too big a step for him. All you can do is lead a horse to water, yes? Anyway . . ." She took out a pen. "I want to tell him this, okay? So—how do you say in Greek— 'I'm free, you're free'?"

Danielle and I glanced at each other and I said, very slowly so Lili could write it down, *"Egó eémay eléftheri, eseé eésay eléftheros."*

"Thanks," she replied. And smiled, more than a little embarrassed. "Probably for the best."

※

Out on the sea, it was impossible not to remember that night in June when Theológos had met our ship and ferried us out to Livádi for the beginning of it all. I could see in Danielle's eyes that she was thinking the same thing, and she smiled and touched my hand.

When we rounded the headland of Livádi Bay, we could see The Beautiful Helen ablaze with lights and hear the music from its jukebox sailing out to us across the waters. In the center of the bay, the black schooner was still resting at anchor.

Poditós didn't say much, but when we docked and were standing on the little stone pier, he muttered, "Eh, Thomá!" and put his arms around me.

After Poditós walked away down the beach, we stood and looked at The Beautiful Helen. It was full of customers, and their chatter came echoing down to us with the music. I could see Theológos serving, the ever-present dish towel draped over his shoulder. I could also make out the young French girl and her father sitting with friends at two joined tables, celebrating her birthday, a burst of their laughter pealing out into the night.

Danielle and I were standing at the edge of the water, right next to the pier. As it happened, this was nearly the exact spot where we had made that attempt, nine years before, to walk on water. Suddenly the evening came back to me with such clarity that I could almost taste it, could almost feel my hand once again clutching Danielle's.

The place had been a madhouse. A bouzouki orchestra, in those days made up of musicians from Livádi (now long since gone on to better things, such as fatherhood and boat building) was on the bandstand, and the usual lines of planks, barrels, and cinder blocks had been set up to make tables and benches on the beach. Theológos was stripped down to his undershirt, sweat glistening on his face and chest, serving dinner, making change, and toiling with Eléni at the stove and counter, while his little sons and Eléni's relatives, imported from the mainland for the evening, were dashing back and forth among a seething mass of revelers that must have numbered, even in those untrammeled days, a hundred or more.

I had spent the previous month pining for Danielle from afar, unable to muster the courage to go up to her either in Skála or at her little house on a cove just outside the port to ask her for a date of some sort. But I had talked incessantly about the possibility to friends, like a fourteen-year-old at his first high school dance, full of bravado but pinioned against the wall by a fear of rejection.

Two of these friends were Alíki and her husband, Andréas, the Athenian architect. They had been very sympathetic to my cause, but, as Alíki later told me, were becoming bored to death with my inaction. So, when she and Andréas learned that I would be at the *paneyíri*, they had taken it upon themselves to drag poor reclusive Danielle out there with them, almost making their purchase of two of Danielle's icons contingent upon her coming. And they had told neither of us of their plans.

When I arrived at the *paneyíri*, I was horrified to see Danielle sitting with them. But Alíki quickly slid over, nearly shoving Andréas off the end of the bench to make sure that the only place I could sit would be between her and Danielle.

I don't remember any of the things Danielle and I said as we sat squeezed together on the bench, shouting to be heard above the music and utterly butchering the French and English languages, but my impression is that we never stopped talking and never, for at least the next couple of hours, turned away to speak to anyone else. I don't believe we ate much either. But we did drink a lot of retsina.

What followed has since passed into legend among those who were at the *paneyíri*. To this day, Alíki still talks about it and remembers that it was Andréas who made the suggestion, but I insist that the idea was mine, that I—intoxicated with the proximity of Danielle's body, heady with the spell of her throaty French accent, her green, almond-shaped eyes and gold-flecked auburn hair, with those beautiful breasts resting loosely within her blouse—had suggested that if there had ever been a moment for walking on water, here on this island of revelations and miracles, then this was it.

Whoever said it, Danielle had instantly agreed. "Yes," she said, "me, too, I believe so!" and at that moment I knew that I was gone, hopelessly head over heels in love.

The two of us rose as one and made our way—somewhat unsteadily—down to the sea. Alíki and Andréas began telling the others around them what we intended to do, and by the time we reached the water's edge, the bouzoukis had stopped playing and a crowd was gathering to watch and urge us on. Among them was Theológos, face florid with the excitement and success of the evening, pounding his hands together along with the others. Even Eléni had emerged from her citadel to see what was going on.

As I stood there holding hands with the woman I loved but had yet to even kiss, listening to the rhythmic clapping and chanting of the onlookers behind us, I could feel myself already levitating. And for a brief moment, I had the mad sensation that we could actually do it.

Danielle looked at me, equally certain about the attempt, and squeezed my hand. Then we took our first step out upon the water, which was gleaming like black polished marble in the windless night.

At this part of the beach, immediately next to the little pier where the caïques dock, the sea bottom is covered with rocks of varying sizes, many of them loose and all of them slippery.

Danielle and I managed about three steps (under the surface) and then fell, not ingloriously, into the water, laughing and embracing each other, while my cigarettes and drachma notes, which, Alíki told me later, I had adamantly refused to give her to hold, bobbed up beside us. We stumbled out of the sea to thunderous applause, shirts and jeans plastered to our bodies.

Naturally, we had to dry off, and naturally, Alíki insisted that I take Danielle to my little house on the hill to do so. She and Andréas even accompanied us most of the way to make sure we actually got there.

Inside, in the bedroom, I took off my shirt and she slipped off hers, and we looked at each other and laughed. She raised her arms, and we embraced, our wet bodies at once cold and hot, and we fell upon the bed, where, for the first time, I tasted her lips against mine.

Now, here we were again at that same spot on the beach looking up at Theológos and his tavérna. Eléni was no longer within, the tamarisk tree had been cut down, and it was not, I finally had to admit, a tavérna called The Beautiful Helen, but rather *Ee Oráya Théa*, The Beautiful View. And apparently it was going to go on thriving without me.

Nearby, the children were splashing in the water trying to make it shine with the same phosphorescence as it had alongside Poditós's caïque.

And what should have been a moment full of sorrow and regrets over the shattering of all my dreams didn't seem so bad at all.

I took Danielle's arm. "Remember trying—"

She smiled. "To walk on water?"

"Yeah," I said, shaking my head. "Well, at least we gave it a shot!"

"Yes we did."

She reached out to touch my face. "You're tired."

I smiled. "I feel great!"

As the children ran on ahead of us along the water's edge, we walked toward the far end of the beach, where we could see the lights of Théo's new snack bar.

Earlier that evening, in Skála, a little boy had brought us a message. Théo had called to ask us to stop by for a complimentary drink. Some friends who wanted to see us would be there.

"One friend special," said the boy.

"Who?" I asked.

"Melyá?"

As we walked away from The Beautiful View, I turned to Danielle.

"You know," I said. "I think I'm going to call that school up in northern Greece about a teaching position. The woman who told me about it said it has a theater."

"Really?"

"Sounds too good to be true, I know, but—just for a second—imagine . . ."

Reckonings

As it turned out, the school in northern Greece did have a theater—well, actually, a very tiny assembly hall with a raised area at one end, but I managed to persuade the administration to cough up enough money for some front lights and a tiny dimmer board, and we were in business.

Like Danielle, Melyá refrained from pointing out that she'd told me so, but when we met that evening at Théo's Place, she nevertheless had the self-satisfied smirk of a cat who'd just swallowed a very large canary—in this case every shred of pride I had left. In her munificence, she forgave me for all the wrongs she imagined I had done her while never for a moment backing off from her basic belief that I had plotted with Theológos to force her out of the partnership, all evidence to the contrary.

We have since become even closer friends than before. In fact, she has read the beginnings of this book and just called from Greece to say, "Thomáki, you haven't changed! You tell wonderful stories, but you're always making things better than they were. I kiss you!"

Returning to Patmos took a while. Mainly because of my commitments at school and the jobs I was getting writing about northern Greece for publications such as Frommer's and Fodor's, but also because I didn't want to have to face Theológos again.

Eventually I made my way back, ostensibly to restock the stores that were carrying my books on the history of the island. But really it was just to be able to rest once more in the bosom of this place that will obviously never—witness this book—leave me.

※

The changes that had been wrought in Skála were apparent even before my ship reached the harbor. Hundreds of lights from new shops and restaurants glittered along the waterfront, and rooftop signs, some lit from below, advertising recently built hotels and rooming houses could be seen sprinkled throughout the town. And now, not only was the pier able to accommodate both a cruise ship and the monstrous car ferry that had brought me from the mainland, but two other tourist lines had their vessels anchored outside the harbor waiting for a berth. There was also, I learned the next day, a fleet of hydrofoils called Flying Dolphins ready to speed visitors with little time but lots of money to and from the nearest islands with airports.

On the dock and on the road approaching it, a mass of private cars, many of them with foreign license plates, clogged the entrance to the boarding area. In the crowd that had packed itself around the ferry's twin gangplanks, I saw only a few faces that I knew.

Eventually, I found the taxi driver Melyá had sent to meet me, a young man with short black hair flecked with gray, pale skin, bloodshot eyes, and a three-day stubble. After we had cleared the congestion in Skála and were barreling along the newly asphalted road to Livádi, he told me he was from Athens and had come to Patmos with his wife and children just for the summer, because the air and sea were so clean, and there was so much work.

"Next year," he said, "maybe I open a restaurant!"

I bit my tongue.

In the square of Upper Livádi, Melyá, Magnus, Jens, and Magnus's latest girlfriend were waiting for me at a table outside Alékos's newly expanded café.

They were all reassuringly the same: Melyá as vivacious as ever, still blond, her skin glowing and wrinkle-free; Magnus, with his hearty grin, stalwart as a defensive tackle; Jens as sallow, unshaven, and near-death from nicotine and alcohol as he had always been; and even the girl was in her Nordic freshness and model-like beauty, a near carbon copy of her eternally youthful predecessors. And her name, too, was Anna.

It took only a moment for me to realize who was missing.

"Lili?" I asked.

"In Oslo," said Magnus. And laughed. "With Mémis!"

"No!"

"You remember those collages he used to make, with seashells and ropes and sand and things? Well, she's found him a gallery!"

"Really?"

"All the rage," muttered Jens, with a sardonic grin that revealed a pair of missing molars.

I told them our news: Danielle, too, had found a gallery and had been hard at work preparing an exhibit. The school's seventy-acre campus was just outside of Thessaloníki, a magnificent seaport with a long tradition of fostering the arts, and as people found out about my theater background, I was also beginning to get back into the professional theater, having been asked to do lighting for a ballet company at the city's annual Festival of the Arts in October. Meanwhile, our children were happily attending a tiny international school huddled in a corner of the same campus where I worked, a ten-minute walk from our house. All in all, it seemed to have been a wonderful move. Granted, I didn't have much time to write anymore, not with a full day of classes and the student Drama Club to take care of, but. . . .

A line of cars rumbled through the square and disappeared down the road toward the beach. I looked at my watch. It was nearly midnight.

"They're going to Theológos's," said Magnus.

I glanced at Melyá and quickly looked away. But she'd caught me.

"I go," she said. "Sometimes. Too many people."

"There's a new restaurant in the middle of the beach," said Magnus. "Run by a family from Athens. It's okay."

"Mostly, though, we're at Théo's Place," Melyá continued.

"How is he? The same?"

Melyá looked at me. "Théo?"

"Theológos. *O Ladós.*"

She paused for a moment and then said, "A lot of things have changed."

"Yes?"

She smiled. "You'll see."

I looked at Magnus and Jens. They seemed to have no idea what she meant.

"I think his sons are cute," said Anna.

※

It took me a couple of days to get up the courage to make my way down to the beach and the tavérna. I had business to take care of in Skála and Hóra, I said, for my books. At night I was too tired. Melyá's house was on the hillside overlooking the valley just outside the village of Upper Livádi, and it was a twenty-minute walk down and about a half-hour back. So in the evenings we sat on her terrace and talked, while I wallowed in the pleasures of being back in Livádi at night, the warm breezes fragrant with thyme and oregano, the stars reaching right down to the horizon in every direction.

In the mornings I was awakened by the soft, cascading sound of animal bells pouring down the mountainside behind the house as rivulets of goats meandered in search of the last meager pickings of spring. There was also the occasional dissonant caw of a crow or a blessedly far-off rooster, and the chain-sawing of a distant motorbike on its way up from the beach. But most of all, there was the silence, and the silence behind that, holy and immense, awesome, as it was in the beginning and had been, world without end.

※

On the third morning, as I stood in front of Melyá's waiting for her to turn her son's Jeep around, I again savored the panorama of Livádi spreading out below me. In sharp contrast to Skála, the valley was almost exactly the same as it had been the first summer I'd arrived, crisscrossed by the same low stone walls, donkey paths, and dry riverbeds, dotted with the same tiny, whitewashed churches and farmhouses (including our Comnénus!), with the same sproutings of cacti and fig, lemon, and olive trees greening the brown and rocky landscape. And beyond it, as the sun rose over an eastern promontory, the dark blue early morning waters of the Aegean sparkled, as always, with promise.

We went to Skála first for the mail and some shopping, and then Melyá drove back out to Livádi and down to the beach. This road, too, once so treacherous for Evripídes's *aeropláno,* was now smooth with a dusty covering of asphalt. I looked over at the house on the hill. Somebody was on the terrace, but I couldn't tell who. I asked about Varvára and Stélios. "The same!" shouted Melyá as she swerved to avoid the bus heading up from the beach.

Seconds later we were in the tiny parking area just before Theológos's. Melyá dropped me off and immediately drove on to meet friends at Théo's Place.

I stood for a moment off to the side looking at the tavérna. It seemed much smaller than before, as if, when I had last seen it, I had been a child. Melyá had said that things had changed, but other than my own inner perspective, I could find no evidence of it. Even the plastic table coverings seemed to be the same.

Then, emerging from the shadows within, I saw Lámbros and Sávas.

For a moment, I didn't recognize them.

Both had become young men. Lámbros, once the smallest, was now the larger of the two, with the stocky build of a soccer player. His blond hair had turned a soft brown, but his cheeks were still rosy with his mother's high coloring, and his eyes a limpid blue. Sávas, as if to compensate for his lack of bulk and for the long, dark lashes that he had inherited from his mother, was attempting to grow a mustache like his father's, but it was as yet simply a never-shaven wisp on his upper lip.

They both recognized me, though, and quickly dropped what they were doing to come out and embrace me. Melyá had told them when I was arriving, so my appearance wasn't a complete surprise.

Seconds later, Démetra joined us, not hugging me like the boys—she had a wooden spoon in one hand and a dish towel in the other—but grinning and pounding me on the shoulder, face flushed like a schoolgirl's. While the gold tooth was still in place, the one next to it was gone, the first gap in many that were to come.

Accompanying her was a young woman with short, reddish-blond hair, wide apple cheeks, cornflower-blue eyes, and a smile so warm and infectious that it made the gold in Démetra's tooth look dull. She was wearing a brand-new checkered apron and drying her broad hands on a dish towel.

Lámbros grinned, chest puffing slightly, and took her arm. "This is my girlfriend, Nicoletta," he said, "from Amsterdam. Nicoletta, this is Thomá."

"Ah!" she answered in perfect English. "So you're the famous Thomá!"

"Well . . ."

"We run the tavérna now," said Lámbros proudly.

"Really?"

"Yes," said Sávas. "Our father has taken his retirement!"

I looked over their shoulders.

"He's inside," said Lámbros, lowering his voice. I peered into the shadows, but could see nothing.

"Do you think I should say hello?"

They looked at one another, then at me.

"If you want to," said Sávas.

I looked again and this time thought I could make out the faint form of someone seated on a chair in a corner by the door.

A group of tourists wandered up from the beach and took a table.

"Excuse me, Thomá," said Sávas.

"See you later?" asked Lámbros.

"For sure," I said.

When I stepped inside, it took a moment for my eyes to adjust to the light. Then I saw him. He was seated at a table in the corner, a vantage point from which he could survey all that went on outside as well as at the display cases and cash box. So he must have spotted me the moment I arrived. He was wearing a wrinkled white shirt and an old pair of brown pants, and he had flesh-colored plastic flip-flops on his feet. In one of his hands was a string of worry beads with a blue-eyed ceramic medallion on one end, proof against the evil eye.

"Yásoo, Thomá," he said when I entered.

His voice was soft, and his smile subdued. His mustache had quickly become almost entirely gray, and his brown hair was thinning on top. He looked like he hadn't been out in the sun yet that summer.

He inquired after my health and that of Danielle and the children. But he didn't suggest that I sit or offer me a drink.

I asked how he was.

"Good, Thomá," he said. And smiled, making a gesture at the tavérna. "The boys do all the work now."

"And your caïque?"

"Now and then," he said. And paused. "But it's too much, Thomá. Too much. You will see."

He started clicking his worry beads, flipping them over in that thick paw of his, and looked out at the sea.

"Tee na kánoumeh, Thomá!" he said. "What can we do!"

He lapsed into silence, and it quickly became clear that he had left me, just like that.

After a moment, I mumbled that I had to go to meet Melyá. He nodded, and I walked away.

Outside, I said good-bye to the boys and started out for Théo's Place. A few steps down the road, I came face to face with a sign I hadn't noticed before, chained to the branches of a tamarisk tree just beyond the tavérna. It was fashioned out of the flat stern of an old caïque and had obviously been painted and put there by the boys.

On it was a bright orange, golden-rayed sun rising out of an azure sea. And below, in a flowery, dark blue script outlined in white was the name *"Ee Oráya Avghí."*

The Beautiful Sunrise.

I looked back at the boys. They were standing in the midst of the tables watching me, hands on their hips, grinning.

Beyond them, I could see Theológos seated in the shadows.

He was still staring out at the sea, flipping the worry beads over and over. Otherwise, he was as motionless as if he had been carved in stone.

※

Ithaca

When you start on the journey to Ithaca,
wish that the way will be long,
full of adventures, full of knowledge.
Of the Laestrygonians and the Cyclops,
of furious Poseidon, do not be afraid,
such as these on your journey you will never meet
if your thoughts soar, if only the finest
feelings touch your spirit and your body.

The Laestrygonians and the Cyclops,
and wild Poseidon you will never meet,
unless you keep company with them in your soul,
unless your spirit itself brings them forth.

Wish that the way will be long.
Many summer mornings may there be
when you enter harbors new to you,
with such pleasure, such joy,
and stop at Phoenician markets
to buy their finest merchandise,
mother of pearl and coral, amber and ebony,
and voluptuous perfumes of every sort,
as many voluptuous perfumes as you possibly can;
to many Egyptian cities may you go,
to learn and learn again from the learned.

Always in mind you must have Ithaca.
Arriving there is your purpose, your destiny.
But don't hurry the voyage, not at all.
Better to let it last for many years;
and old at last to anchor at the island
rich with all that you have gained along the way,
not expecting riches to be given you by Ithaca.

Ithaca gave you the beautiful journey.
Without her you would not have ventured on the way.
But she has nothing to give you now.

And if you find her poor, Ithaca hasn't mocked you.
As wise as you have become, with such experience,
by now you will have understood what is meant by Ithacas.

—C. P. Cavafy

Extra Helpings

The Menu of The Beautiful Helen

As in most Greek tavérnas and quite a few Greek restaurants, the menu offered at The Beautiful Helen had little to do with what had actually been prepared. Preprinted by an ouzo company for advertising purposes and handed out free to restaurant owners, it was a generic list of scores of items that *might* be available but usually weren't. So, like most establishments, we encouraged our customers to come inside and look.

But if I had had my own menu, it would have looked something like this:

APPETIZERS (*Orektiká*)
YOGURT, CUCUMBER, AND GARLIC DIP (*Tzatzíki*) [page 206]—Strained yogurt mixed with peeled, grated cucumber, garlic, and olive oil, with the distinctive addition of a small amount of white pepper for elegance.
EGGPLANT DIP (*Melitzánosaláta*) [page 208]— Roasted, peeled eggplants pureed with olive oil, lemon juice, and garlic. Chopped walnuts enhance its delicious, smoky flavor.

EGGS (*Avgá*)
TZATZÍKI OMELET (*Omeléta meh Tzatzíki*) [page 210]—A piping hot omelet filled with a dol-

lop of chilled *tzatzíki*. Available by special
order only.

SEAFOOD (*Thalasiná*)

MUSSEL PAELLA (*Meédia meh Rízi*) [page 212]—
A poor man's mock paella with canned mussels, rice, green pepper, chopped tomatoes,
onion, and garlic cooked in lots of chicken
bouillon.

PASTA (*Zeemariká*)

SPAGHETTI ALLA CARBONARA (*Makarónia meh
Avgá kay Báykon*) [page 214]—Spaghetti with
eggs, bacon, evaporated milk, freshly ground
black pepper, and grated cheese. Available by
special order only.

MEAT (*Kréas*)

CHILI CON CARNE (*Meksikánikoh Fasólia meh
Keemá kay Tomátess*) [page 216]—Authentic
Tex-Mex chili made with ground beef, red
kidney beans, green peppers, and genuine chili
powder direct from New York.

GREEK MEATBALLS (*Keftédes*) [page 218]—
Meatballs spiced with grated onion, cinnamon, cumin, cayenne, and chopped parsley,
deep-fried until golden brown.

MEATBALLS IN EGG-LEMON SAUCE (*Youverlákia
Avgolémono*) [page 220]—Ground beef mixed
with rice, parsley, mint, and spices, and cooked
in an egg-lemon sauce until fragrant.

STEAK AU POIVRE (*Bon Filéh meh Triméno Pipéri
kay Konyák*) [page 222]—Filet mignon crusted
with coarsely ground black, white, and green

peppercorns and accompanied by a cognac-and-butter sauce flambéed with the drippings. By special order only.

CHICKEN (*Kotópoulo*)

CHICKEN RETSINA (*Kotópoulo Retsináto meh Stafília*) [page 224]—Golden-brown pieces of sautéed chicken smothered in a sauce of resinated white wine and halved green grapes.

EGYPTIAN CHICKEN WITH SPAGHETTI (*Ayiptiakó Kotópoulo meh Makarónia*) [page 226]—Boiled and boned chicken baked with spaghetti in a sauce made of the chicken broth, lemon, oil, cinnamon, cardamom, and turmeric.

CHINESE CHICKEN WITH CUCUMBERS (*Kinésiko Kotópoulo meh Angúri*) [page 228]—Cubed chicken breasts cooked in a sauce of garlic, ginger, white wine, soy sauce, and chile peppers and topped with thinly sliced cucumbers.

CURRIED CHICKEN (*Kotópoulo Kári*) [page 230]—Chicken thighs cooked in a curry sauce flavored with yogurt, almonds, and raisins.

SPECIALTY OF THE HOUSE

TOM'S MOUSSAKA (*Moussaká Thomá*) [page 232]—The classic Greek dish specially adapted from various versions sampled in Athens, Crete, and New York. Made with layers of deep-fried potatoes, zucchini, and eggplants; a meat sauce spiced with cinnamon, allspice, red wine, and oregano; and an egg-béchamel topping delicately seasoned with cinnamon and grated *kaséri* cheese.

The Recipes

These are for the above items as well as many mentioned elsewhere in the text.

First, the ones on the menu, then those in the text.

YOGURT, CUCUMBER, AND GARLIC DIP
(Tzatzíki)

This is a variation on one of the most popular Greek hors d'oeuvres. It is traditionally made with either chopped or grated cucumber, no pepper, and a generous amount of garlic and olive oil. It is the addition of white pepper that makes all the difference. As always, the longer you wait for the flavors to mingle, the better—at least 4 hours in this case, refrigerated.

6 SERVINGS

1 pint fat-free yogurt (see Note below)
2 cloves garlic, crushed
A hefty dash of white pepper
1–2 tablespoons olive oil or other oil
1 medium cucumber, peeled
½ teaspoon salt

1. Place the yogurt in cheesecloth or a fine-mesh strainer or one lined with a paper coffee filter and let drain at least 3 hours or overnight in the refrigerator. This will produce what the Greeks call *stragisméno*, strained, yogurt—deliciously thick and creamy, even if fat-free.
2. Combine the strained yogurt, crushed garlic, white pepper, and olive oil to taste and refrigerate.

3. Grate the peeled cucumber into a colander and sprinkle generously with the ½ teaspoon of salt. Let drain in a bowl or on a plate for about 30 minutes. Rinse, squeeze dry, and combine with the yogurt mixture.

4. Let the flavors of the mixture blend in the refrigerator for at least 4 hours.

5. Serve as a dip with celery, carrots, flat breads, crackers, or, as the Greeks do, with chunks of bread.

Note: Most national brand-name American yogurts, Dannon for one, are so thoroughly homogenized that they will not release their liquids, so use a high-quality local product, such as those found in health food stores.

EGGPLANT DIP
(Melitzánosaláta)

This is the Greek equivalent of guacamole and is a tasty alternative to the latter, accompanied by the usual tortilla chips or pita toast. The Greeks eat it by the forkful or on chunks of bread. By far the most delicious way of preparing it is to grill the whole eggplants over a wood or charcoal fire until the skin blackens and splits and the inside is soft. The eggplant's naturally smoky flavor is enhanced to a heavenly degree.

These days, most people, including the Greeks, bake or grill the egg-plant in a very hot oven.

The addition of walnuts, which I learned about while living in the north of Greece teaching school in the years following the summer of the tavérna, adds a definite elegance to the dish.

MAKES ABOUT 2 CUPS OF DIP

2–3 medium eggplants (about 3 pounds)
3–6 tablespoons olive oil
2 cloves garlic, crushed
2 tablespoons chopped parsley
Salt and white pepper to taste
2–3 tablespoons lemon juice or white vinegar
½ cup coarsely chopped walnuts (optional)

1. Preheat the oven to 375° F.
2. Wash the whole eggplants, dry them, and puncture them with a fork in several places.
3. Bake for an hour or until soft and the skin shrivels.

4. Let cool, cut off the ends, and peel, washing off the bits of charred skin under running water. At the same time, squeeze to get rid of the often bitter juices.

5. In a bowl, mash the eggplants with a fork until roughly pureed. Thoroughly stir in the oil with the fork, then the garlic, parsley, salt, and pepper. Add the lemon juice to taste, a teaspoon at a time. Finally, if desired, add the chopped walnuts.

6. Serve, as the Greeks do, with chunks of bread, or with chips and crackers of various kinds.

Note: A variation on the above, as with guacamole, is to add chopped tomatoes and onions.

TZATZÍKI OMELET
(Omeléta meh Tzatzíki)

This originated on a lazy day with nothing much in the refrigerator. It combines a piping hot omelet with a cold yogurt-cucumber-garlic filling.

SERVES 2

2–3 tablespoons Yogurt, Cucumber, and Garlic
   Dip (*Tzatzíki*) (page 206)
4–6 medium eggs or egg whites
4–6 teaspoons water
Salt and white pepper to taste
Cooking spray

1. Have the cold *Tzatzíki* ready.
2. In a bowl, beat together the eggs with an equivalent number of teaspoons of water and the salt and white pepper.
3. Heat an omelet pan coated with the cooking spray until it is very hot and quickly pour in the beaten eggs. Shake the pan in a vigorous horizontal motion while lifting the edges of the cooked layer of eggs to let the raw egg slide under.
4. Continue this until the eggs are set. Then add 2–3 tablespoons of the cold *Tzatzíki* in the middle, bisecting the cooked eggs on a line perpendicular to that made by the handle.
5. Grasping the handle underneath with your left hand, lift the pan off the heat and slide the

omelet down toward a serving plate, rolling it over on itself as it gently falls out of the pan onto the plate.

6. Cut in two and serve with toasted pita bread and sliced tomatoes sprinkled with oregano.

MUSSEL PAELLA
(Meédia meh Rízi)

This was created during one of those bleak Lenten periods on Patmos when not even a frozen chicken was to be found in the island's butcher shops and groceries. But there were some canned mussels from Denmark, and fresh squid, neither of which are prohibited during the fast because they don't contain blood. Of course, lobster and shrimp don't either, but this is a poor person's paella.

For the purpose of simplicity and to avoid too many "and/ors," we will speak here only of mussels. But both mussels and squid can be used. Or only squid, which must be boiled until tender and then cut into pieces.

SERVES 4–6

     2 tablespoons olive oil
     1 medium onion, chopped
     1 clove garlic, crushed
     1 green pepper, seeded and chopped
     1½ cups uncooked rice
     Strong chicken broth plus reserved mussel
        liquid, enough to make 3 cups
     ½ teaspoon turmeric
     2 medium tomatoes, chopped
     Freshly ground black pepper
     12 ounces canned mussels, liquid reserved
     ¼ cup chopped parsley

1. In a deep, wide skillet or large saucepan, heat the olive oil; sauté the onion and crushed garlic in the oil until they are golden.

2. Add the green pepper and sauté 2 minutes.
3. Mix in the rice and, stirring almost continuously, sauté a further 3 minutes.
4. Meanwhile, in a separate saucepan or in the microwave, heat the 3 cups of chicken broth and reserved mussel liquid until just simmering. Remove from the heat.
5. Add the turmeric (or other saffron-colored powder—or real saffron for that matter!) to the broth.
6. Place the tomatoes on top of the rice and add the hot mussel-and-chicken broth, pouring it in all at once. Add a generous amount of freshly ground black pepper.
7. Bring to a boil, stir once, cover, and simmer gently for 15 minutes.
8. Place the mussels on top of the rice, along with the chopped parsley, re-cover, and simmer a further 10 minutes or until the rice is cooked and all the liquid has been absorbed.
9. Mix the mussels and parsley into the rice and serve.

SPAGHETTI ALLA CARBONARA
(Makarónia meh Avgá kay Báykon)

As mentioned earlier in the text (see pages 36–41), this recipe is derived from versions made in Rome and Milan. You can use real heavy cream if you wish, but in trying it out on Patmos, one of the things I discovered was that evaporated milk, when simmered down, makes a much "creamier" texture than the real stuff.

The secret in making a perfect carbonara lies in its final assembly, when the temperature of the pot and the pasta must be hot enough to cook the egg mixture into and around the strands of spaghetti but not so hot as to scramble them nor so low as to leave them under-cooked.

SERVES 4

¼ pound bacon, roughly chopped
1 clove garlic, crushed
4 eggs
¼ cup evaporated milk, or more
A generous amount of freshly ground black
     pepper
1 pound spaghetti
½ cup dry white wine
A pinch of dried oregano
8 tablespoons butter or margarine, cut in pieces
1 cup freshly grated Parmesan cheese

1. In a skillet, slowly sauté the bacon until it is lightly browned but still soft, adding the crushed garlic after the bacon's fat has begun to melt. When browned, set the skillet and its contents aside, off the heat.

2. In a bowl, beat together the eggs, ¼ cup of evaporated milk, and black pepper.

3. Cook the spaghetti in a large quantity of boiling salted water until just al dente.

4. In the meantime, add the wine and oregano to the bacon in the skillet and boil it down over medium heat until almost entirely evaporated.

5. While the spaghetti is draining, quickly add all the butter to the pot in which it has cooked, swirling it around. Immediately return the spaghetti to the pot and toss it briefly. Add the bacon with its drippings and toss again, briefly.

6. Add the egg mixture and gently stir and turn into the spaghetti until the mixture has thickened slightly and been partially absorbed by the pasta.

Note: If the previous steps are followed in relatively rapid succession, the heat from both the pot and the hot spaghetti should be sufficient to thicken the eggs. However, if not—and if necessary—the contents can be placed over an extremely low heat during this last step, but precautions must be taken to avoid the very real risk, if the heat is too high, of ending up having to serve the spaghetti with tiny, bite-sized omelets clinging to its strands.

7. Finally, add the Parmesan cheese and mix it in briefly, but thoroughly, with the rest.

CHILI CON CARNE
(Meksikánikoh Fasólia meh Keemá kay Tomátess)

This is a combination of numerous "authentic" chili recipes I have encountered over the years. So, like chili itself, it is a mix of a great many things, hopefully the best of the best.

SERVES 4

3 tablespoons vegetable oil
1 large onion, roughly chopped
2 cloves garlic, minced
1 green pepper, seeded and roughly chopped
1 tablespoon ground cumin
3 tablespoons chili powder
1 pound ground beef, or 1 pound chuck steak
    preferably roughly chopped in a food processor
3 cups beef bouillon
1 (14.5-ounce), can crushed tomatoes or 1 pound
    chopped fresh tomatoes
1 cup dry red wine
1 teaspoon dried basil
1 teaspoon dried oregano
1 teaspoon celery seed
1 small bay leaf
$\frac{1}{4}$ teaspoon cayenne pepper, or to taste
1–2 tablespoons yellow cornmeal to thicken
1 (16-ounce) can red kidney beans, drained, or
    2 cups cooked red kidney beans
Salt to taste

1. Heat the oil in a skillet, add the onion and garlic, and sauté over low heat until golden brown.

2. Add the green pepper, cumin, and chili powder and sauté for 2 minutes, stirring constantly.
   This frying of the spices with the other ingredients will release more of their flavor, much in
   the way Indian cooks do with their curries.
3. Add the meat, breaking it up with the flat side
   of a wooden spoon, and stir, cooking until the
   meat is a grayish color. If you try to brown it it
   will become far too dry.
4. Transfer the beef mixture to a large pot and
   add all the remaining ingredients except the
   cornmeal, kidney beans, and salt.
5. Bring to a boil, reduce the heat, and simmer,
   uncovered, until the sauce is thick and shiny,
   about 1 hour. To thicken further, sprinkle in
   1–2 tablespoons of cornmeal and cook a further 5 minutes, stirring to prevent the cornmeal from forming lumps.
6. Add the kidney beans and cook another 5–10
   minutes. Add salt. Let sit as long as possible—
   preferably overnight in the refrigerator—and
   remove and discard the bay leaf before serving.

GREEK MEATBALLS
(Keftédes)

Good either as marble-sized hors d'oeuvres or, when walnut-sized or larger, as a main course. Try to serve these hot or at least warm, otherwise the congealing fat in the meat will make them increasingly less appetizing.

There are infinite varieties throughout Greece. The ones that I prefer are those that I remember Eléni making, flavored in the spicy, Levantine style of northern Greece. I have been told, but never come across proof, that keftédes *were on the menus of classical Athens.*

SERVES 4–6

1 pound beef or lamb, ground several times over
   or kneaded or pounded in a mortar until
   almost a paste.
2–3 slices of bread, crusts removed
1 tablespoon oil (vegetable or olive)
4 tablespoons grated onion
4 tablespoons finely chopped parsley
4 tablespoons finely chopped fresh mint, or
   3 tablespoons dried mint
½ teaspoon dried oregano
½ teaspoon ground cumin
¼ teaspoon ground nutmeg, or ½ teaspoon
   ground coriander
½ teaspoon ground cinnamon
⅛ teaspoon cayenne pepper (optional)
Salt and black pepper
½ cup red wine, sweet or dry
Flour for dusting

1. Once the meat is ground or pounded to a paste, moisten the bread, squeeze the liquid out, and mix into the meat with all the remaining ingredients except the flour for dusting. Shape into walnut-sized balls and dust with the flour.
2. Fry in vegetable oil in a skillet or in a deep fat fryer until brown on the outside but still moist within.

Variations on this recipe include the addition of a few pine nuts and mint in place of the parsley.

Also, the meat mixture can be shaped around skewers, fried or grilled, and served either as brochettes or wrapped in pita bread as a variety of gyro (pronounced "yeéro").

Finally, the meatballs can be served in a tomato sauce of your choosing (usually a simple one of tomato paste, water, cinnamon or cumin, and a little lemon juice) and served as a main course with rice.

MEATBALLS IN EGG-LEMON SAUCE
(Youvarlákia Avgolémono)

This is a classic Greek dish that even the most ordinary tavérnas always seem to get right, no matter how pedestrian the rest of their food. It is the inclusion of fresh dill in the meatballs and the quality of the egg-lemon sauce that really make the difference.

SERVES 4–6

The Meatballs:
A large pot of beef stock
1 pound ground beef or lamb, pounded or
    kneaded into a pastelike consistency
⅓ cup uncooked short-grain rice
½ cup chopped or grated onion
2 cloves garlic, crushed
1–2 tablespoons finely chopped fresh dill
½ cup finely chopped parsley
1 teaspoon dried oregano
1 egg
Salt and white pepper to taste

The Egg-Lemon Sauce:
3 large eggs
Lemon juice (1–2 lemons, depending on how
    tart you want the sauce)

1. In the pot, bring to a boil enough stock to cover the meatballs.
2. Meanwhile, in a bowl, mix the ground beef together with the uncooked rice, onion, garlic, chopped dill and parsley, oregano, and egg.

Season with the salt and pepper and knead until thoroughly blended.

3. Shape into balls 1–2 inches in diameter.
4. Carefully slide the meatballs into the boiling stock, cover, and simmer for 35–40 minutes, until the meat and rice are well cooked, adding more liquid, if necessary, to keep the meatballs covered.

Note: While the meatball "soup" can be prepared beforehand, the egg–lemon sauce should be made and stirred in just before serving.

5. In a medium-sized bowl, beat the eggs and lemon juice together until frothy.
6. To this egg mixture, very gradually add 2 cups of the meatball broth, beating continuously with a whisk to keep the eggs from congealing into lumps.
7. Lower the heat under the cooking pot and pour in the egg mixture, continuing to stir vigorously until the soup has thickened. Do not allow it to boil. Serve immediately.

STEAK AU POIVRE
(Bon Filéh meh Triméno Pipéri kay Konyák)

This recipe is the result of a decades-long quest to re-create the steak au poivre *I had as my first evening repast in Paris, France. Of course, the following will never approach what is now a near-mythic meal, but I am pleased to offer it anyway.*

SERVES 1

1 (1½-inch-thick) steak, preferably filet mignon
¼ teaspoon each coarsely ground green, white,
 and black Tellicherry peppercorns, or to taste
2 tablespoons canola oil
2 tablespoons butter
2 tablespoons chopped spring onion
⅓ cup beef broth
3 tablespoons cognac

1. Several hours before cooking, wash the steak and press the ground peppercorns into both sides, forming a crust. Let sit in the refrigerator, covered.
2. Melt the 2 tablespoons oil in a heavy skillet until very hot but not browning.
3. Sear the steak on both sides, then cook 3–5 minutes on each side, depending on how rare you want it.
4. Transfer the steak to a heated platter and keep warm.
5. Pour out almost all the fat from the skillet and add 1 tablespoon butter. Melt the butter and stir-fry the onion for 30 seconds. Add the

broth and use the liquid to scrape the steak residue from the bottom of the skillet.

6. Heat the cognac and add to the skillet, flaming it. Swirl until the alcohol is burned off. Bring the liquid to a boil and reduce to about 2 tablespoons.

7. Swirl in the remaining 1 tablespoon of butter.

8. Pour the sauce over the steak and serve with baked, French-fried, or oven-roasted potatoes and a green salad.

CHICKEN RETSINA
(Kotópoulo Retsináto meh Stafília)

This was invented when I was staying at a friend's house on Mykonos. Finding that there was nothing to eat but some rice, a chicken in the freezer, grapes hanging over the door, and a large wicker bottle of retsina in the pantry, I came up with the following, truly a gift of the Greek gods, particularly considering how hungry we were!

SERVES 4–6

1 (4–5-pound) frying chicken, cut into pieces
2–4 tablespoons flour
Salt and white pepper to taste
2 tablespoons vegetable oil for frying
2 tablespoons chopped onion
1–2 cups retsina
1–2 cups seedless green grapes, halved

1. Wash and dry the chicken and dredge with the flour and salt and pepper.
2. In a large skillet, heat the oil and fry the chicken pieces gently until golden brown.
3. Remove and set aside on paper towels to drain. Keep warm.
4. Put a little more oil in the pan if necessary and sauté the chopped onion until translucent.
5. Return the chicken to the pan, add 1 cup of the retsina, and simmer gently until the chicken is cooked, about half an hour, adding more retsina if necessary.

6. Add the halved grapes to the sauce and boil down rapidly until the sauce thickens slightly and the grapes are softened.
7. Serve with rice cooked in chicken broth and a chilled bottle of—what else?—retsina.

EGYPTIAN CHICKEN WITH SPAGHETTI
(Ayiptiakó Kotópoulo meh Makarónia)

This was adapted from Claudia Roden's superlative A Book of
Middle Eastern Food *(Penguin, 1970), by far the best cookbook I
have found for making use of the indigenous culinary ingredients of
the eastern Mediterranean region. It is also one of the best cookbooks
I have ever come across, period.*

*For the tavérna, I used a much compressed, less time-consuming
method than the one in Ms. Roden's book.*

SERVES 4–6

> 1 large chicken, cooked (preferably, but not nec-
> essarily, boiled in water seasoned with salt and
> white pepper, ½ lemon, ½ teaspoon turmeric,
> and a cracked cardamon pod. If this is not
> done, make a sauce with: 1½ cups chicken
> boullion; salt and white pepper to taste;
> 1 cracked cardamom pod; ½ teaspoon turmeric;
> and juice of ½ lemon; and set aside)
> 1 pound thin spaghetti (No. 8 or 9)
> 2 tablespoons canola oil
> 1 teaspoon ground cinnamon plus more for
> sprinkling

1. Preheat the oven to 350° F.
2. Skin and bone the chicken and cut into 1-inch
   pieces.
3. Cook the spaghetti until almost al dente.
4. On the top of the stove, heat the 2 tablespoons
   of oil in a large oven- and flame-proof dish

until very hot. Throw in the very well-drained spaghetti and stir-fry over medium heat until well coated.

5. Remove half the spaghetti and spread the rest over the bottom of the dish.
6. Spread the chicken pieces over this layer of spaghetti, sprinkle with the teaspoon of cinnamon, and cover with the rest of the spaghetti.
7. Pour in the reserved sauce or seasoned chicken broth (see above), sprinkle with a little more cinnamon, and cover the dish.
8. Bake in the 350° F. oven for 20–30 minutes. Unmold onto a platter and serve either hot or cold.

CHINESE CHICKEN WITH CUCUMBERS
(Kinésiko Kotópoulo meh Angúri)

This was adapted from a marvelous food-processor cookbook I was lucky enough to find in an Athens bookstore, Jean Anderson's Processor Cooking.

The original calls for such exotic ingredients as fresh ginger, sherry, and celery. In Greece at the time, ginger was nonexistent except in powdered form, sherry was nearly as rare and prohibitively expensive, and celery could be found only in the winter but, because of a lack of water, thrived solely as leaves. So I used the substitutes listed below.

SERVES 4

2 tablespoons cornstarch

1 tablespoon plus ¼ cup retsina (or sherry, if you've got it)

1 egg white, beaten until frothy

A pinch of salt

2 whole chicken breasts, skinned, boned, and cut into 1-inch cubes

1 large clove garlic, peeled and crushed

¼ teaspoon powdered ginger, or 2 teaspoons fresh ginger, peeled and chopped

¼ cup soy sauce

½ teaspoon crushed dried red chile pepper

4 tablespoons peanut or other cooking oil

2 medium onions, thinly sliced

6 spring onions, including tops, cut into 1½-inch lengths

2 medium cucumbers, peeled, halved lengthwise, and cut into very thin slices

1. In a large bowl, combine the cornstarch and the tablespoon of retsina, the beaten egg white, and the salt. Add the chicken cubes to the mixture and let stand at room temperature 30 minutes.

2. Meanwhile, in a small bowl or cup, combine the rest of the retsina with the garlic, ginger, soy sauce, and chile pepper, and set aside to make the sauce at the end.

3. When the chicken is ready to cook, heat the peanut oil in a wok or large skillet over high heat until a small test piece of the chicken sizzles in it. Add the chicken with the egg-white mixture and stir-fry, separating the pieces until a golden brown—about 3 minutes.

4. Remove the chicken and drain on paper towels.

5. Pour off all but 2 tablespoons of the oil remaining in the wok. Add both the onions and stir-fry for about 1 minute.

6. Pour in the soy sauce mixture, add the stir-fried chicken, and cook over high heat for about 2 minutes to reduce and thicken, gently stirring and mixing all the while.

7. Add the sliced cucumbers, stir-fry 1 minute, turn off the heat, and cover for another minute before serving. Waiting too much longer, say 15 minutes, will cause the cucumbers to lose their crispness entirely, not a complete catastrophe—it happened all the time in the tavérna—but a shame. Serve with boiled rice.

CURRIED CHICKEN
(Kotópoulo Kári)

This is adapted from one of my favorite curries, a very aromatic Murghi (or Mughlai) Korma, that was perfect for making in Greece because of the inclusion of yogurt, almonds, raisins, cloves, and cinnamon, near staples in Greek cooking, albeit in desserts!

SERVES 4

5 cloves garlic, crushed
1 (½-inch piece) fresh ginger, peeled and
    chopped, or ¼ teaspoon ground ginger
4 tablespoons blanched, slivered almonds
2 tablespoons water
2 pounds chicken thighs, skinned and pricked
    all over with a fork
2 tablespoons oil, or more
2 onions, thinly sliced
¼ teaspoon ground cloves
¼ teaspoon ground cinnamon
1 teaspoon ground cumin
⅛ teaspoon cayenne pepper
5 cardamom pods, cracked
½ cup yogurt
½ cup heavy cream or evaporated milk
1 bay leaf
1 tablespoon golden raisins
1 teaspoon garam masala
Salt to taste

1. Put the garlic, ginger, almonds, and water into a food processor or blender and switch on and off until blended into a paste. Two hours

before cooking, rub the paste into the chicken thighs and set aside.

2. In a heavy skillet, heat the 2 tablespoons oil, add the sliced onions, and slowly fry until brown, at least 15 minutes. Remove the onions from the skillet and set aside.

3. Add half the chicken thighs to the skillet and carefully fry over medium heat until golden brown on both sides but not burned. Remove and set aside. Fry the remaining pieces in the same manner.

4. If necessary, add a little more oil and stir-fry the cloves, cinnamon, cumin, cayenne, and cardamon pods for 2–3 minutes until brown and the oil begins to separate from the mixture.

5. Add 1 tablespoon of the yogurt. Stir-fry for about 30 seconds. Add another tablespoon of the yogurt and stir-fry. Keep adding in this manner until all the yogurt has been incorporated.

6. Return the onions and chicken to the pan along with any liquids, add the ½ cup of cream and the bay leaf, cover, and simmer gently for 20 minutes.

7. Add the raisins and some water if necessary to prevent burning, cover and cook for another 10 minutes, or until the chicken is done.

8. Remove the bay leaf, stir in the garam masala, salt to taste, and serve with fluffy white rice.

Note: A nice accompaniment to this or any other curry is Greek Tzatzíki (page 206), which has nearly the same ingredients as the Indian condiment raita *and makes one wonder if the recipe wasn't brought there (or back) by Alexander the Great.*

TOM'S MOUSSAKA
(Moussaká Thomá)

This is a compilation of various recipes for moussaka that I have picked up during my travels around Greece, the best of which I owe to a superb cook named Socrátes, in whose tiny tavérna in Rethymnon I worked for a summer before venturing into my partnership on Patmos.

Finding a good moussaka in a regular (i.e., not luxury) Greek restaurant is about as difficult as locating the lost continent of Atlantis. There are two main reasons for this. First, in most places, the béchamel topping either has too much semolina and too few or no eggs or, if it is made with eggs, it is flat from having sat in a food warmer for the better part of a day or more. Second, the oil that has been used to fry the vegetables has not been allowed to drain sufficiently before the moussaka was assembled and baked, rendering it soggy and unpalatable.

The ingredients in a moussaka vary from region to region and often from cook to cook. In some areas, the inclusion of potatoes is a must, in others a sacrilege. This also goes for the kinds of spices used.

There are four processes involved: 1) the salting, frying, and thorough draining of the vegetables, better done the night before; 2) the preparation of the meat sauce (called bolonése *by the Greeks), also better done the night before; 3) the making of the béchamel topping; 4) the assembling and baking.*

Finally, please note—if you haven't already—that the accent is on the last syllable: moussaKA.

SERVES 12

The Vegetables:

3 medium eggplants, cut crosswise into
   ¼-inch-thick slices
4 medium zucchini, cut lengthwise into
   ¼-inch-thick slices
Cooking oil for frying
3 medium potatoes, cut crosswise into
   ¼-inch-thick slices

The Meat Sauce:

1 onion, chopped
2 tablespoons olive oil
1 pound ground beef
1 tomato, chopped
1 teaspoon ground cinnamon
¼ teaspoon allspice
3 tablespoons tomato paste
½ cup red wine
1 teaspoon dried oregano
3 tablespoons finely chopped parsley
Salt and pepper to taste

The Béchamel Topping:

4 tablespoons butter
4 tablespoons flour
2 cups boiling milk
Salt and white pepper
1 tablespoon grated *kaséri* cheese
A pinch each of ground cinnamon and grated
   nutmeg
2 beaten eggs

4 tablespoons grated *kefalotíri* (or Parmesan)
   cheese

The Assembly and Baking:

1. Salt the eggplants and zucchini, allowing them to drain in colanders for at least ½ hour to draw out any bitter juices.
2. Wash off the salt under running water and squeeze out any remaining juices.
3. Dry thoroughly on paper towels and either deep-fry or pan-fry in a generous amount of cooking oil until golden brown.
4. Drain on paper towels and then, if you wish, keep them overnight in colanders in your refrigerator.
5. Fry the sliced potatoes and drain the oil on paper towels. (These are better prepared the day of the cooking.)
6. To make the meat sauce, sauté the onion over medium heat in the oil until golden.
7. Add the beef and sauté over medium heat until grayish brown, mashing down the clumps with the back of a wooden spoon.
8. Add the rest of the sauce ingredients and simmer uncovered at least 30 minutes.
9. Let sit until cool. The longer it sits, the better the flavor. Overnight in the refrigerator is best.
10. For the topping, in a saucepan, melt the 4 tablespoons of butter over low heat and stir or whisk in the flour a tablespoon at a time until smoothly blended.
11. Gradually stir in the milk, whisking constantly until the sauce is thick and smooth. Stir in the grated *kaséri* cheese and cinnamon and nutmeg.
12. In a bowl, beat the eggs well and slowly add a

little of the hot sauce to warm the eggs up without cooking them.

13. Add the egg mixture to the sauce and, stirring constantly, cook over very low heat for a couple of minutes or until very thick.

14. Taste and add salt, pepper, and spices if necessary.

15. Preheat the oven to 350° F.

16. Grease a 15 x 11 x 3-inch metal or ovenware casserole. Cover the bottom of the casserole with a layer of the fried eggplant, then add layers of the rest of the ingredients in the following order: the potatoes, the meat sauce sprinkled with 3 tablespoons of the grated *kefalotíri* cheese, and the zucchini.

17. Spread the hot béchamel sauce evenly on top and sprinkle with the rest of the grated cheese.

18. Bake for 45 minutes to 1 hour, until the béchamel is golden brown on top.

19. Remove from the oven and let sit for at least an hour to cool slightly and set. If you cut into it too soon, it will come out on the spatula as a gooey mess rather than with the lemon-meringue-pie consistency that it should have. Serve with a nice light green salad of shredded romaine lettuce and spring onions.

WILD GREENS
(Hórta)

During World War II the Patmians were reduced to foraging the countryside for wild greens as practically their only source of sustenance. Fortunately, these are rich in vitamins A and C as well as calcium, iron, potassium, and other nutrients.

Some varieties of hórta can be very bitter, while others are delicate in taste and absolutely delicious. In Greece, local tavérnas serve both kinds and you just have to take your chances. The very best, to my mind, are chickory (rathíkia), black mustard greens (vroóva), and arugula (róka). Then, of course, there are those other varieties also readily available in U.S. markets, such as dandelion greens, escarole, kale, collard greens, and beet leaves.

To Cook:

1. Bring a large pot of unsalted water to a boil.
2. Meanwhile, wash the greens (about ½ pound per person) thoroughly, leaf by leaf, to get rid of any sand or dirt in the leaf crevices.
3. Cook the greens in water to cover until soft, about 20–40 minutes, depending on the type used.
4. Drain, cool, and, if desired, roughly chop.
5. Serve cooled or at room temperature and sprinkle with olive oil and lemon juice or vinegar. The addition of a slice of feta cheese on top or at the side makes this simple dish wonderfully redolent of Greece in the spring.

One-Fish Bouillabaisse

An easy dish to make, in spite of the apparently formidable list of ingredients. I invented and often prepared it on my two-burner electric stove in the house on the hill.

*The best fish to use is one that is indigenous only to the Mediterranean: the scorpion fish (*rascasse *in French and* scorpína *in Greek). It is a highly prized type of rockfish that has a very tasty firm, white flesh and, perhaps more important, a high gelatin content, perfect for enriching fish soups. That said, I have found that any saltwater fish with a similarly firm white flesh, such as halibut or grouper, can be used with almost equally delicious results.*

The bouillabaisse can be served with fresh bread spread with garlic butter or, if you wish to commit a certain form of heresy (which I often do) against a true Marseillaise bouillabaisse, you can put into the soup, along with the tomatoes, seasonings, and fumet, several potatoes, peeled and cut into eighths, boiling them for 10 minutes before adding the fish and olive oil and raising the heat.

This, in effect, would turn the version above into one from Provence, which is not so bad either.

There are two steps involved in preparing a bouillabaisse. First, the making of a fumet or fish stock, and then the actual bouillabaisse.

SERVES 4

The Fumet:
1 medium onion, chopped
1 carrot, chopped

2 tablespoons chopped celery
$\frac{1}{2}$ cup chopped parsley
3 tablespoons olive oil
2 cups water
$\frac{1}{2}$ cup dry white wine
6 peppercorns
1 teaspoon dried thyme
$\frac{1}{2}$ bay leaf
A twist of lemon rind
Fish trimmings: head, tail, and fins

The Bouillabaisse:
$\frac{3}{4}$ cup olive oil
1 large onion, chopped
5 cloves garlic, crushed
3 large tomatoes, chopped
2 tablespoons tomato paste
1 bay leaf, crumbled into small pieces
1 teaspoon fennel seeds, crushed
$\frac{1}{4}$ cup chopped parsley
1 piece of dried orange peel
A pinch of turmeric
6 medium potatoes (optional), cut into
    1-inch cubes
Salt and freshly ground black pepper to taste
4 pounds fish (rockfish, halibut, grouper), scaled,
    cleaned, and cut into large pieces
About 3 cups fumet (add water to fumet, if nec-
    essary, to make about 3 cups)

1. In a saucepan, gently sauté over low heat the
   chopped onion, carrot, celery, and parsley in
   the olive oil for 5 minutes.

2. Add the water, white wine, peppercorns, thyme, bay leaf, lemon rind, and the fish trimmings. Bring to a boil and let simmer for 30 minutes.

3. Strain immediately through a fine sieve (otherwise it tends to become bitter) and keep refrigerated until ready for use.

4. In a large casserole, heat ½ cup of the olive oil over medium flame and in it sauté the onion and garlic until the onion is soft and transparent.

5. Add the tomatoes, tomato paste, crumbled bay leaf, fennel, parsley, orange peel, turmeric, potatoes (if using), salt, and a generous amount of freshly ground black pepper. Stir the ingredients together until thoroughly mixed.

6. If the flesh of the fish you have chosen is very firm, place the pieces on top of the vegetables and seasoning mix, sprinkle with the remaining ¼ cup olive oil, add the fumet with enough water, if necessary, to make about 3 cups, and bring to a rapid boil, which should be sustained for 15 minutes (see Note below).

7. If the fish is more delicate and could thus tend to disintegrate while boiling, add it later to the broth, giving it just time enough to cook.

Note: The essence of a good bouillabaisse is in the consistency of its broth, in the emulsification of the olive oil with the water and wine. This can be achieved only by keeping the bouillabaisse boiling as vigorously as possible for the entire length of its cooking time, which should be about 15 minutes, certainly no less and not much longer.

ELÉNI'S VEAL STEW
(Moschári Stifádo)

This is my approximation of the delicious stifádo that Eléni used to make while she was still presiding over The Beautiful Helen.

Stifádo, whose distinctive ingredient is tiny whole onions, is ubiquitous in Greece and is used as a basic recipe for stewing all kinds of flesh, including tongue and octopus. But I won't go any further here than veal.

SERVES 4

¼ cup olive oil
2 pounds veal, cut into 1-inch cubes
1 pound small white or pearl onions, peeled and
    kept whole
¾ cup tomato paste
3 cups water
1 clove garlic, minced
2 carrots, sliced
2 potatoes, cubed
1 teaspoon ground cinnamon
Salt and freshly ground black pepper to taste

1. In a large pot, heat the olive oil and brown the cubes of meat on all sides over high heat. Remove to a plate.
2. Put the onions in the pot and stir-fry over medium heat until golden. Remove to a plate.
3. In the pot, stir in the tomato paste and water. Bring to a boil and return the meat and onions to the pot along with the minced garlic. Simmer the stew, covered, for about 1½ hours.

4. Add the sliced carrots, cubed potatoes, cinnamon, salt, and pepper.

5. Re-cover the casserole and cook for another ½ hour or until the meat and vegetables are tender.

SPAGHETTI SARA SLEEPING

*As mentioned in the text, this was named to honor the evening that
our new baby, Sara, slept straight through our evening dinner hour
for the first time since her birth some two months before. I had
thrown the dinner together before this miraculous event and only
named it afterward. That night, on our house on the hill, there was
very little left in the larder except some spaghetti, dried mushrooms,
a shriveling zucchini, evaporated milk, and numerous cans of powdered baby formula (not included . . .)*

SERVES 4–6

2 medium zucchini, cut into matchstick-sized
   pieces
Salt
12 or more dried black wood-ear mushrooms
   (2 rounded palmfuls)
1 pound spaghetti, linguine, or fettucine
2 tablespoons oil, olive or vegetable, or more
2 tablespoons finely chopped onion
2 cloves garlic, minced
1/2 cup white wine
1/2 cup chicken broth
1/2 cup butter, cut into chunks
1/2–3/4 cup evaporated milk
1–1 1/2 cups freshly grated Parmesan cheese
Freshly ground black pepper to taste

1. Put the zucchini into a colander or strainer,
   sprinkle with salt, and set aside so that the
   juices will sweat out. Then wash off some of
   the salt, squeezing out the rest of the juices.
   Dry with paper towels.

2. Put the dried mushrooms to soak in a sufficient amount of warm water for about 30 minutes. Drain and roughly chop.
3. Meanwhile, in a large pot, bring salted water to boil for the pasta.
4. In a skillet, heat the oil and stir-fry the chopped onion over medium heat until soft, about 3 minutes.
5. Add the zucchini and garlic. Stir-fry for 1 minute and remove.
6. In the same skillet, add a little more oil if necessary and sauté the chopped mushrooms for 2 minutes.
7. Add the wine and chicken broth to the skillet and bring to a boil, reducing the liquid by about one-quarter. Return the sautéed zucchini, onion, and garlic to the skillet and remove from the heat.
8. Cook the pasta according to the package directions until al dente.
9. Drain the pasta.
10. Meanwhile, put the cut-up pieces of butter into the hot pot and swirl to cover the bottom. Return the pasta to the pot and mix it with the butter.
11. Add the evaporated milk and, over low heat, occasionally turn the pasta over to allow the strands to absorb the thickening milk, about 3 minutes.
12. Just before serving, add the Parmesan cheese and freshly ground black pepper and mix in.
13. Add the zucchini mixture from the skillet, heat, and serve immediately with a green salad.

KÓLIVA
(Ta Kóliva)

Kóliva is traditionally served at funerals or memorial services for the dead, with a small portion being reserved for the deceased to take along on the journey. This aside, it is also absolutely delicious and makes a wonderful dessert for vegetarians and meat-eaters alike.

This recipe comes unaltered from the papadiá *(priest's wife) of "Livádi," and serves about fifty parishioners in very small quantities.*

Pomegranate seeds are traditional, but dragées, which are edible, can be used.

> 2 pounds wheat berries
> 3 pounds sesame seeds
> 1 cup slivered almonds
> 1 tablespoon ground cinnamon
> 2 cups raisins, golden, black, or both
> 1¹/₂ pounds powdered sugar
> Pomegranate seeds or silvered dragées (optional)

1. In a large pot, bring to a boil enough lightly salted water to cover the wheat berries by 3–4 inches. Add the wheat and simmer, uncovered, for 2 hours.
2. Meanwhile, toast the sesame seeds over low heat until beige (but not browned, otherwise they become bitter).
3. When the seeds have cooled, grind them to a powder in a mill or food processor.
4. When the wheat has cooked and cooled, mix in the powdered sesame seeds, slivered almonds, cinnamon, and raisins.

5. Place the mixture on a large plate and flatten into the shape of a cake about 2 inches high. Sprinkle all over with the powdered sugar and smooth out with a piece of wax paper.
6. Cut a piece of cardboard in the shape of a cross and press it into the top of the cake. Using a sharp, pointed object such as a nail, outline the shape of the cross into the cake.
7. Remove the cardboard and fill the outlined indentation with the pomegranate seeds or silvered dragées. Also use the dragées to decorate the outside edges of the cake.
8. Clean the powdered sugar from the rim of the plate and serve. The portions are usually doled out on napkins, but in Athens, they are offered in small paper sacks decorated with a cross.

Memorial services for the dead are first held forty days after the funeral. There may be another service six months later, but most of the time, they are held annually. In the third year, the bones of the dead are taken from the ground and placed in an osteofilakiá *(ossuary), thus making room in the limited cemetery grounds for the more recently deceased.*

It is interesting to note that Greek Sephardic Jews serve kóliva *not to mark deaths but to celebrate births, thus further reaffirming the deep regenerative, life-giving symbolism of the wheat grains and pomegranate seeds.*

Kalí Óreksi!
(Good Appetite!)

Recipe Index

249

About the Author

TOM STONE has pursued a multifaceted career as a novelist, travel writer, historian, and stage- and screenplay writer. Simultaneously, he has had a very successful career in the professional theater as a director, lighting designer, and stage manager.

After his graduation from Yale in 1958, he spent the next decade working as a stage manager and assistant director for Jerome Robbins and Harold Prince on the original productions of *She Loves Me, Funny Girl, Fiddler on the Roof,* and *Cabaret,* as well as on the now-legendary efforts of Robbins's American Theatre Laboratory.

Deciding to give a career in writing one last chance, Mr. Stone went to Greece for a summer and ended up living there for twenty-two years, principally on the islands of Patmos and Crete and near the mainland capital of northern Greece, Thessaloníki, where he taught English at the American-owned preparatory school Anatolia College.

While in Greece, he wrote and published his first novel, *Armstrong,* and numerous books and articles about living abroad. These include *The Essential Greek Handbook, Greece: An Illustrated History, Patmos,* and *Tom Stone's Greek Food & Drink Book.*

Mr. Stone now lives in Southern California, where he is writing a second novel and patiently waiting for one of his six optioned screenplays to actually be made into a movie. He and "Danielle," a successful painter in Greece, have recently concluded an extremely amicable divorce. Meanwhile, their two children are pursuing their own lives in and out of university. But the four of them are and always will be very much a family.